COMPUTER SCIENCE, TECHNOLOGY AND APPLICATIONS

AUGMENTED REALITY

DEVELOPMENTS, TECHNOLOGIES AND APPLICATIONS

COMPUTER SCIENCE, TECHNOLOGY AND APPLICATIONS

Additional books in this series can be found on Nova's website under the Series tab.

Additional e-books in this series can be found on Nova's website under the e-book tab.

COMPUTER SCIENCE, TECHNOLOGY AND APPLICATIONS

AUGMENTED REALITY

DEVELOPMENTS, TECHNOLOGIES AND APPLICATIONS

RAYMOND HUGHES

EDITOR

nova publishers

New York

Library of Congress Cataloging-in-Publication Data

Augmented reality : developments, technologies and applications / Raymond Hughes, editor.
pages cm. -- (Computer science, technology and applications)
Includes bibliographical references and index.
ISBN 978-1-63482-902-1 (hardcover)
1. Augmented reality. I. Hughes, Raymond, 1968- editor.
QA76.9.A94A94 2014
006.8--dc23

2015016753

Published by Nova Science Publishers, Inc. † New York

CONTENTS

PREFACE

Augmented reality (AR) is a technology that enables the user to see the real world, with virtual objects superimposed upon or composited with the real world. This book includes chapters focused on the following: the methodology of AR software for educational purposes; the use of augmented reality applications in the area of music education and music therapy; medical AR (in which the virtual entity is medical data); the role of AR in consumers' augmented experiences; and AR for cultural heritage, meaning the developments in multimedia technology to facilitate the learning experience in cultural heritage with the aid of improved user interaction methods.

Chapter 1 – A variety of computational technologies are available to enhance the teaching-learning process and although some of these applications have received attention for their effectiveness, they have not yet been widely adopted by teachers. One such example is augmented reality (AR) applications. Part of the lack of implementation of AR is that thus far, no industry-approved best practices have been established to ensure that AR applications fulfill educational goals. In order to support the widespread adoption of this technology, this paper addresses the possibility of non-expert users (teachers) developing AR software for educational purposes. The author presents a software development methodology to guide these users. This paper describes the methodology, explaining its implementation and designing a case study involving non-experts.

Chapter 2 – This chapter aims to discuss the use of augmented reality (AR) applications to the area of music education and music therapy. Three applications will be presented that have been developed by the authors, tested by experts in music education and children in schooling process (Music-AR), and music therapist and children with Cerebral Palsy in Music Therapy

(GenVirtual and MusicandoRA). It is a multidisciplinary research involving different professionals: engineers, computer scientists, musicians, therapists and educators. In addition to the scientific contributions generated in this work, deserves its technological contribution, given that the three applications are available for free use.

Chapter 3 – On-patient medical data visualization is desirable in several practical situations such as surgical planning and medical training. Currently, it becomes possible with the augmented reality, a technology which enables the visualization of patient virtual anatomy at the location of the real one in a conventional display. In this chapter, the author presents a multiview marker-free augmented reality environment for on-patient medical data visualization which supports: volume rendering, advanced methods for real and virtual data composition, rigid and non-rigid tracking and additional features such as occlusion. To achieve real-time performance, the most critical algorithms take advantage from the graphics processing unit to reduce processing time. Moreover, the multi-view architecture of the application includes an augmented reality glasses and two RGB-D sensors, one to capture the observer (i.e., physician) and the other to capture the observed structure (i.e., patient region of interest). The results obtained from an evaluation of the proposed environment highlight that it runs in real-time and provides good visual quality for the final augmented scene.

Chapter 4 – In the actual hypercompetitive and unsure economic contest firms must necessarily make attention to new opportunities given by the social exchanges, i.e., the growth of internet connection in store by smartphones, in order to increase the chances to succeed or simply to survive in the market. Nowadays consumers strongly need to express themselves, to create relationship, and to have value exchanges. Therefore firms could gain success by setting up an emotive and passionate dialogue with them, by means of a new interactive marketing approach. New technologies and social media allow continuous contacts between firms and users and, consequently, they improve mutual knowledge. Even the customer experience changes and evolves thanks to the support of new technologies, into and off stores. While e-commerce apparently threatens traditional trade, stores realize that competitive prices, suitable goods selection and additional services are not enough to attract and hold consumers back. In this light, recent studies underline as users are more likely to buy when they have involving interaction with brands and engagement in stores. Thus, capitalising on user's digital knowledge, firms try to exploit this trend to their advantage. In this context, augmented reality, that is the application of virtual elements in a real dimension, conceived as strategic tool, supports the creation of brand engagement through immersive customer experiences and improve firms' turnover. In spite of this, the phenomenon is not immune to problems and limits which, after a thorough analysis of augmented reality both from a theoretical and empirical point of view, will be extensively encountered and discussed in the present chapter.

Chapter 5 – Augmented Reality (AR) provides an entertaining means for displaying 3D reconstructions of ancient buildings *in situ* for cultural heritage. Finding the pose, position and orientation, of the user is crucial for such applications since this information will be used to define the viewpoint that will be used for rendering the models. Images acquired from a camera can be used as the background for such augmentations. To make the most out of this available information, these images can also be utilized to find a pose estimate. This paper presents contributions for vision-based methods for estimating the pose of the user in both indoor and outdoor environments. Keyframe-based tracking algorithm is presented. Continuing with vision-based approaches, Kinect sensor was also used to find the pose of a user for *in situ* augmentations making use of the natural features in the environment. Skeleton-tracking was also found to be beneficial for such applications. The paper then investigates combining the vision based estimates with measurements from other sensors, GPS and IMU, in order to improve the tracking accuracy in outdoor environments. Finally, several AR applications are presented that make use of these methods. The first one is for *in situ* augmentation for displaying historical columns and augmenting users, the second is a virtual visit to an ancient building and the third is a game which can also be played inside the augmentation of the building in the second application.

In: Augmented Reality
Editor: Raymond Hughes
ISBN: 978-1-63482-902-1

Chapter 1

DEVELOPMENT AND EVALUATION OF AUGMENTED REALITY EDUCATIONAL APPLICATIONS

Valéria Farinazzo Martins[1]*, Marcelo de Paiva Guimarães[2] and Cláudio Kirner[3]
[1]University Presbiterian Mackenzie , Brazil
[2]Open University of Brazil-UNIFESP/Faccamp's Master Program, São Paulo, SP, Brazil
[3]Federal University of Itajubá, Brazil

ABSTRACT

A variety of computational technologies are available to enhance the teaching-learning process and although some of these applications have received attention for their effectiveness, they have not yet been widely adopted by teachers. One such example is augmented reality (AR) applications. Part of the lack of implementation of AR is that thus far, no industry-approved best practices have been established to ensure that AR applications fulfill educational goals. In order to support the widespread adoption of this technology, this paper addresses the possibility of non-expert users (teachers) developing AR software for educational purposes. We present a software development methodology to guide these users.

* email: valeria.farinazzo@mackenzie.br

This paper describes the methodology, explaining its implementation and designing a case study involving non-experts.

1. Introduction

Improvements in computer technologies and educational strategies in the last few years have allowed educators to incorporate software in the learning process at schools. New technologies have supported advances in traditional educational environments and these advances have created new ways for students to learn and for teachers to share knowledge [1], [2]. In this context, in which technologies are tools to help students reach learning goals, educational applications should be simple to develop and easy to use. They should also be flexible enough to add new features that can support different student learning styles, diverse teacher strategies, and advanced learning goals.

In order for educational applications to be widely adopted, their use should not require any prior knowledge and should involve minimal teacher and student training. They should be developed with the potential user profile in mind; for example, an application's design could take into account that its users know how to create videos on mobile platforms and share them in repositories such as YouTube. Familiarity with specific tools is common for users when they are exposed to environments where the technologies are naturally relevant, such as creating videos with mobile device, manipulation of videos and pictures on social networks, use of text editors, image capture, sound recordings, etc. [3]. The software's design should also consider the hardware available to its potential users. In many cases, however, web applications have become as powerful as desktop applications, in which case they offer an alternative to achieving hardware and software portability.

The need to make a transition to a technology-enhanced classroom has been increasingly demonstrated through state-wide and international projects in which schools are supplied with computerized technologies. There is a need to immerse students in rich contextualized learning settings [4]. The increasing use of computational technologies in education can be attributed to the emergence of new software tools, the low cost of hardware, and improved educational strategies. Computers are becoming more sophisticated every day, with higher storage capacities, exceptional processor performance, and network communications that have ever-increasing speeds and a global reach. Applications have also dramatically improved, solving increasingly complex problems [5], [6]. Despite the widespread improvements in computer hardware and software, some technologies, such as augmented reality (AR), are rarely used. AR refers to applications which allow users to view real-world environments onto which virtual objects (e.g., 3D/ 2D images, videos, and sound) are superposed [7]. AR applications can be applied to many types of systems in many scientific fields. Perhaps the most exciting application to date is in the educational field, in which AR applications offer fun, interactive features, student autonomy, special devices independence such as glasses or head-mounted display, intuitive interactions, and student involvement [8], [9]. An AR application can assist students during the learning process by, for example, adding virtual objects to a wide range of bi-dimensional images from the microscopic to that of a volcano [10]. Information added by the virtual objects can help students understand real world activities. Figure 1 depicts two examples of educational AR applications that can be used to explain differences between terrestrial and marine animals. In these examples, Figure 1(a) depicts an orca whale that is highly social and has sophisticated hunting techniques and vocal behaviors. Figure 1(b) depicts a giraffe that has an extremely long neck and legs. The 2011, 2012, and 2013 annual editions of the Horizon Report [11] indicated that AR is one of the new technologies that has the ability to influence the nature of education over the next few years.

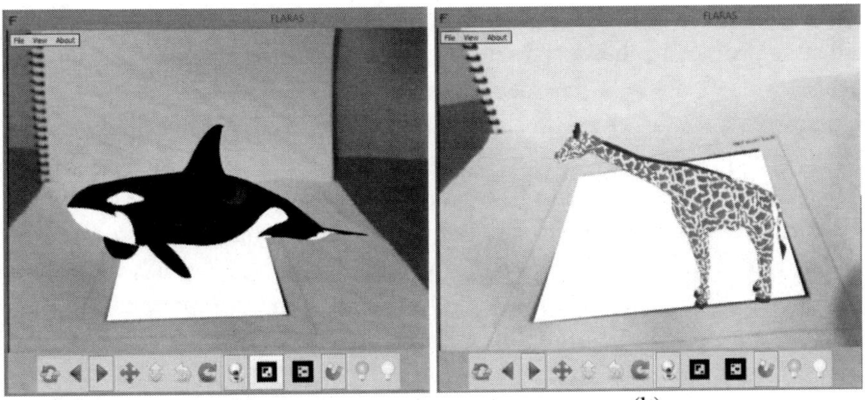

(a) (b)

Figure 1. Augmented reality in an educational context.

AR faces challenges when it comes to widespread implementation because its applications require expert developers. The lack of industry-established best practices with which teachers can develop AR applications has prevented this technology from being adopted on a larger scale. A possible solution to this problem is to provide strategies with which non-expert users can create AR applications without possessing deep technical knowledge. Teachers need an easy-to-use authoring tool with which they can build and adapt AR applications, changing the content and structure independent of specific educational subjects and hardware. The Flash Augmented Reality Authoring System (FLARAS) [12] is such a tool. It is specifically tailored to assist non-expert users with AR application development. This tool allows teachers to develop AR applications for the web with no programming knowledge. It also allows teachers to focus on the educational content rather than the technological aspects of AR. AR is a relatively new field; thus, not many studies have been conducted with a specific focus on how to create AR applications. The main contribution of this chapter is to simplify the design of AR applications by presenting a systematic process with which to guide non-expert users (such as teachers). A case study developed by non-expert users (teachers) is presented to validate this software development process. This AR application was implemented by a teacher (non-expert) using the FLARAS tool during a training course on new technologies in education. (AR was taught as part of this course.) Regardless of whether or not the developers are experts, an efficient software development process for this kind of application is built in the following stages: requirements analysis, design, implementation, and testing. In the requirements analysis stage, it is necessary to know the pedagogical needs of teachers and to link this to a teaching/learning process and user profile. In the design stage, it is essential to choose the tools and technologies that will be needed to fulfill the requirements. In the implementation stage, the AR application is developed. Finally, in the testing stage, the application is run to ensure that it incorporates the established requirements. The remainder of this chapter is organized as follows: section 2 presents information about an authoring tool for augmented reality applications; section 3 addresses the process by which teachers can develop educational AR applications; in section 4, a case study is presented using a development process presented in a previous section, and section 5 presents the conclusions.

2. Authoring Tool for Augmented Reality Applications

There are many people without programming skills, such as teachers, who are interested in developing AR applications. To work around this barrier, some authoring tools provide resources for non-programmers so that they can create their own applications [13]. It is important to mention that, ideally, these applications will be independent of compilers, operational systems, and programming languages and will instead use text editing, configuration procedures, visual interfaces, and tangible actions.

An example of a high-level authoring tool is the Flash Augmented Reality Authoring System [12]. FLARAS is free open-source software available on the Internet at http://ckirner.com/flaras2. It includes support material such as downloadable versions of the tool; tutorials based on texts and videos; FAQs; an e-book; a repository with various online applications, accompanied by their respective projects, open and licensed for the adaptation and creation of derivative works; and information about the software developers. FLARAS has a graphic interface supported by Internet browsers that have installed Adobe Flash Player.

FLARAS can be used with a single marker (a drawn card with a frame and a symbol therein) and is based on the concept of spatial points with stacked virtual scenes containing images, sounds, videos, and 3D objects. Each point can be linked to a list of virtual objects. This feature allows the use of a minimum amount of markers instead of a pack of markers to interact with the application. The student uses just one marker; when he/she clicks over a virtual object (scene 1.1 in Figure 2), the object associated with the scene (in this case scene 1.2) is presented, and so on. These scenes can be enabled or called in sequence, using a mouse click or an interaction marker. Figure 2 depicts the spatial points concept.

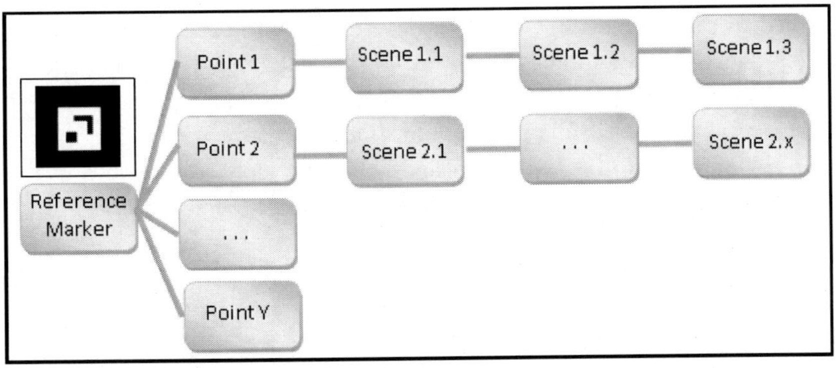

Figure 2. Logical structure of FLARAS tool.

Figure 3 depicts the FLARAS tool interface that allows visual authoring applications. The developer uses this graphical interface to create the software organization (scene graph), fill all parameters, and visualize the virtual objects in real time.

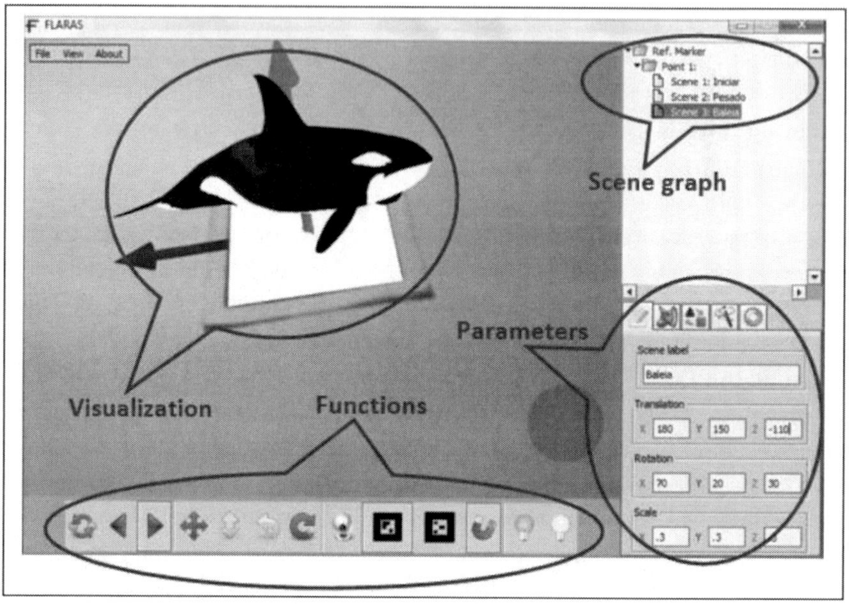

Figure 3. Main FLARAS interface.

This tool is structured and implemented gradually using the design demands of educational applications and the appropriate functionalities for teachers and students. The multimedia resource data to be used can be obtained from internet repositories or developed by the user. Adding sounds, images, and videos should be no problem for digital natives and can be learned quickly by non-digital natives through open training courses. The big challenge would involve the production of 3D objects modeling, but there are already open repositories with thousands of 3D objects, compatible with the tools, which can be downloaded and incorporated into the educational applications [3].

The FLARAS tool is not the only AR software currently available. The following AR tools can be differentiated by the degree of ease with which non-expert users can create material (and also by their limitations):

- ARToolKit [14] is one of the first AR tools that used markers and computer vision. To use it to create AR applications, developers need to have skills in programming in C/C++. Its content design tool eliminates dependence on the programming language and replaces it with descriptions of the virtual objects and their relationships with the real environment.

- DART [15] is a tool implemented on Macromedia Director using a model of a visual type of authorship "drag-and-drop" and an interpreted scripting language (textual descriptions).
- AMIRE [16] is based on a structure that uses component-oriented technology, providing a minimum set of components for demonstration, a collection of reusable resources, and a visual authoring tool.
- ComposAR [13] is an extensible tool for authoring AR applications for non-programming users. It supports a scripting and "drag-and-drop" interface and interprets input and features added by users in real time.
- ARSFG [17] is a software tool for the rapid prototyping of AR applications, based on scene graphs, which enables remote collaboration through an XML-based protocol.
- BasAR [18] is an authoring tool in which the authoring layers are separated into infrastructure, structure, content, performance, and behavior.
- FlarToolKit [19] is a library developed in the ActionScript language. It runs on a majority of web browsers that support Adobe Flash Player. FlarToolKit enables applications to run AR on the Web, providing greater flexibility of access to applications.

3. Development of Educational Augmented Reality Applications

The use of AR as an efficient and effective support tool for the teaching-learning process is a challenge that will require users to overcome various barriers. Initially, it is necessary to identify the content that will be enhanced with the simulation. There is also a need for an easy-to-use authoring tool to facilitate the creation of the software. In addition, it is necessary to adopt an application development process that can address the specifics of AR as well as appropriate teaching methodologies.

3.1. Content Generation

Before creating any content (multimedia objects), it is necessary to define the teacher's educational goals for his or her specific course. With the teaching objectives and technical-pedagogical strategies defined, content creation can be achieved, albeit with considerable time and effort on the part of the creator. To develop such content, computational technical knowledge is needed, as is knowledge of the specific school subject and teaching skills. Because most development tools are not easy-to-use, teachers often lack the confidence to generate applications. Some teachers address this by searching for support staff, but this restricts the technology to only a few institutions and people.

Two approaches are possible with content generation: creating the content oneself or using objects that have already been created (e.g., a 3D model from a repository). The creation of all content requires considerable time (months, in some cases). On the other hand, when one obtains content that has already been created (e.g., images, 3D models, and video), the educational strategy should be designed in accordance with the predetermined characteristics of this content. The developer, however, will have to spend time finding the right content, which may or may not exist. The trend is that in the future, there will be more objects freely available on the internet, since the number of all kinds of repositories has been increasing.

For AR applications to be widely used, the tools must be easy to use, even for complex tasks, thus allowing teachers to focus on the content of their lessons. That way, teachers do not need to have a thorough knowledge of the underlying system (e.g., knowledge of computer graphics, programming languages, how to interface with the operating system, etc.). It is also necessary to create specific educational methodologies for the use of such technology. In addition, all created material should be designed to function within a dynamic new type of classroom, such as using social networks, serious games or Problem Based on Learning (PBL).

Teachers also need to be trained so that they feel secure in their ability to use this technology in the classroom. Open basic courses and training in the creation and manipulation of images, videos, stories, etc. are needed in order to resolve or alleviate the problem related to the diversion of attention of the student in class, using the technology for other purposes. [20], [3].

Technology should improve communication and education management. Technology in education should not be a barrier to the learning process but rather a means of stimulating communication between parents, teachers, and students.

3.2. Software Development Process

The software development process consists of stages and phases of acceptable complexity with the potential to be made operational. In addition to directing the creation of the software, the process followed by developers enables the monitoring and development of the software obtained, seeking efficiency and effectiveness. To accomplish these objectives, the software development process employs techniques and the implementation of support tools for various activities, ranging from requirements engineering to implementation and maintenance of the software system [21], [22].

AR is a young area without enough research (as of yet) to guide the method for developing applications. Due to the peculiarities of AR, such as using markers and mixing real and virtual environment, a suitable development process is required. In spite of belonging to the same category (graphic interface), there are significant differences between AR and conventional graphic applications:

- Conventional graphic applications have a dominant interaction paradigm based on the WIMP model (i.e., the Windows, Icons, Mouse, and Pointer paradigm). On the other hand, AR must develop a dominant interaction paradigm, based on non-conventional interaction, such as markers or gestures.
- The most important activity for conventional graphic applications is considered the task performed by the system. An AR prioritizes the user interaction. These different approaches directly affect the development process.
- Conventional graphic applications are typically based on a run-time, event-driven architecture with which the users trigger actions by events. In an AR application, it is common to have many independent activities running as agents (e.g., image and interaction event processing).

For all the above-mentioned reasons, a specific development process is needed. The software development process presented in this chapter describes four basic interrelated stages that occur in each cycle. The stages are Requirements Analysis, System Design, Implementation, and Evaluation/Test. This process runs interactively, such that the results from one design cycle are used as input in a new design cycle, allowing an incremental refinement through each iteration of the cycle. The advantage of this approach is that it allows for the addition of new functionalities as they become available or known. Another key feature of this process is that it involves the final user early in the system development effort. It requires strict management to conclude such applications without the risk of running the cycle in an indefinite loop. Figure 4 depicts these stages; their descriptions are in the next subsections. The success of the AR application depends on these stages, which require a clear definition of goals and steps taken during each stage.

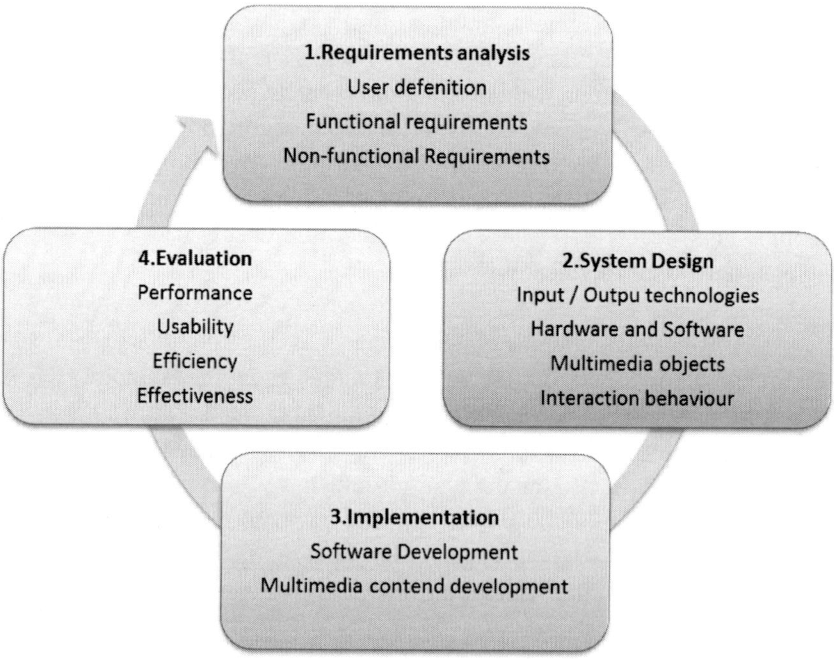

Figure 4. Software development process for augmented reality applications by non-expert users.

3.2.1. Requirements Analysis Stage

The quality of an application is directly influenced by the developer's ability to create a well-defined and effective set of requirements. In a traditional development process adopted by experts, this stage aims to understand the real needs of users and stakeholders. In general, the developers use specific tools (e.g., interviews, questionnaires, user observation, and brainstorming) to gather all requirements. However, the software development process presented in this chapter is directed to non-expert users, especially teachers, who will also be users. Non-expert users must be able to use the tool, which results in a list of requirements for the target application. This step is, certainly, the most difficult stage of the development process because it involves users' and developers' creativity.

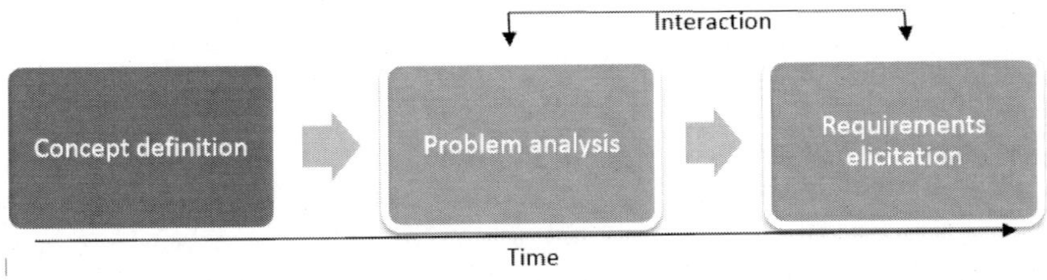

Figure 5. Activities needed to arrive at the requirements list.

Table 1. Questions to help the teacher identify the requirements

Requirements		Questions
Functional	AR application and learning goals	1. What does the application do? 2. Is it a game? Which type? 3. What should the application not do?
Non-Functional	Environment	1. What is the physical environment in which the application will run? The school? The student's house?
	Usability	1. Should the application be easy to use? 2. Should the application be easy to learn? 3. Should the application be easy to memorize? 4. Should the application be fun?
	Users	1. What is the profile of the students who will use the application? 2. With which types of technologies are they familiar?

Figure 5 depicts the activities that the non-expert (teacher) has to complete in order to arrive at the requirements list. Initially, a conceptual overview of how the application will operate is created, taking into account the educational strategy. This activity is used as input in the Problem Analysis stage, which aims to verify whether or not the solution will solve the problem and determines whether or not the problem identified is compatible with the learning goals. Finally, in the last activity, the needs of the application are translated into the application's requirements, which will solve the educational problem [23], [24]. An interactive refinement is applied between the last two activities. In general, the requirements list for AR applications must identify the application's goals, the student profile, and all constraints and describe how the application will work.

The successful generation of requirements will depend on the teacher's capacity to combine learning goals with the authoring tool's features, using a well-defined teaching methodology. In order to simplify and drive this stage, we present a set of questions to be answered by the teachers (Table 1).

3.2.2. Design Stage

This stage aims to address questions related to the technologies that will be employed in the system, including the definition of input and output technologies; the definition of support and computational technologies, both hardware and software; and the definition of the multimedia content, such as 3D objects, textures, markers, and video. In addition, it is also necessary to create the application script, that is, how it will be used in the educational context, including its behavior and supported interactions. A well-defined design minimizes the risk of running the development cycle process in an indefinite loop.

There are tools to assist expert developers during this stage (e.g., UML, MS Visio, DIA, Jdeveloper, and Argo). These tools rely on graphics to visualize or model the artifacts, including code generation. However, as teachers will be using authoring tools to create the applications, we suggest using familiar design tools such as text editors to write the design.

3.2.3. Implementation Stage

This stage should generate prototypes or rapid releases for evaluation. This stage's tasks include:

- Generating two-dimensional images to be used in the AR environment using editing software or performing downloads from free repositories.
- Recording or downloading the audios from a free repository.
- Constructing the markers which allow the interaction with the AR environment or, in the case of markerless applications, constructing the user interaction with the environment.
- Preparing 3D objects that have been designed. This can be accomplished by downloading the 3D objects from free repositories or shaping one's own objects using a 3D object editing program such as Maya [25], 3D Studio Max [26], or Blender [27].

- Building the AR application, associating the virtual objects with markers from the real world.
- Implementing environmental interactions.
- Implementing the interfaces.

3.2.4. Test Stage

In a development process carried out by experts, this stage consists of six steps: evaluation of system performance, usability, security, portability, and reliability, and assessment of the value of the task/application. Testing may be performed in all stages to verify the different activities or artifacts, e.g., to evaluate the loading time of a 3D model or the sound quality. In order to efficiently evaluate applications, it is necessary to involve users early in the development process. This means that the developer must know his or her target audience and establish a close relationship with that audience in order to involve them in the evaluation. It is worth noting that it is extremely important that these projects are located in the target schools, so that the final tests are carried out in the environment in which the application will be used.

It is possible to simplify this stage by tailoring it to fit non-expert users by evaluating only the value and usability of the application, i.e., evaluating the learning benefit it will provide. In order to help users evaluate their own applications, we propose conducting a usability evaluation that finds and reports usability problems during the development process. The earlier problems are identified, the less expensive it is to fix them. Martins, Kirner, and Kirner [28] propose a questionnaire for this class of applications that consists of 53 attributes to measure the usability of AR applications, based on a systematic review about usability criteria of the years 2008 to 2013. The attributes are divided into nine categories: interaction with the system, application interface, performance, sensory and behavioral aspects, motivation and effort, space association, internal aspects, configuration, and general functionality. This questionnaire can serve as a guide for evaluating the usability of educational AR applications; for being very extensive, one can choose the questions that suit the context. These attributes from [28] can be seen in the evaluation of the case study.

During this stage, teachers can also verify the gain in different areas, such as learning, and the capacity of the application of knowledge gained. In order to measure the effect of an AR application, teachers need to take a quality indicator and measure it before and after the evaluation, comparing the learning level before the application use to what it is afterwards. The difference between the two provides an indication of the effect of the AR application. If the teacher aims to measure learning, he/she can use a test or exam or some form of assessment exercise. If a student has to reach a certain level of learning to obtain a "success mark," then the number of marks can be used as an evaluation measure. The teacher can also measure the degree of retention, i.e., how much of the learning the student has retained after the activity is over.

Test results are important to improving the application and the accompanying educational strategies. If students react negatively to an approach, the teacher must try to identify the associated problem, verifying all aspects, including the user profile. These stages of the presented process require the combination of costs and benefits [29] to get precise feedback regarding the insertion of the AR application in the educational context.

4. Developing a Case Study

Dangerous diseases, such as Yellow Fever, Falciparum Malaria, Kyasanur Forest disease, Tanapox, and Mayaro, can be transmitted from monkeys to people.

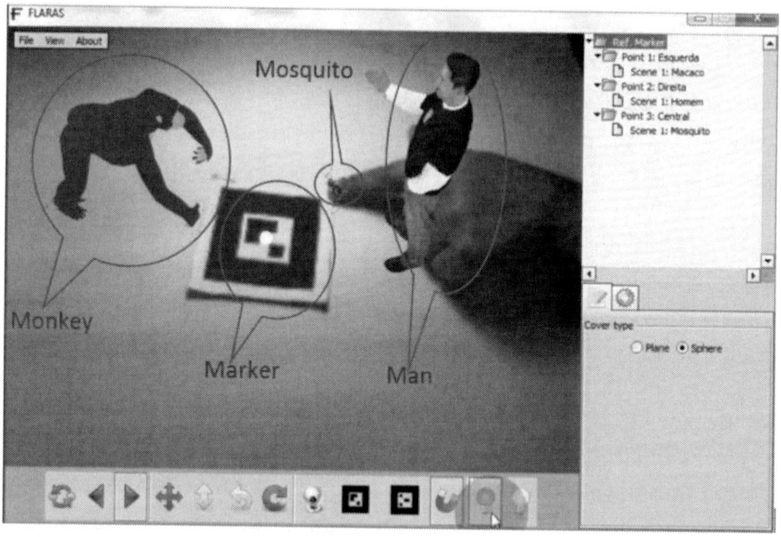

Figure 6. Epidemiological simulation cycle.

We developed a case study to illustrate the interactions between mosquitoes and their hosts (human and non-human primates). This case study was developed following the steps set out by the development process presented in this chapter. Figure 6 shows this AR application, which simulates a mosquito flying and biting the man and the monkey. This mosquito is animated and includes sound. The user can manipulate the marker to observe the simulation from different viewpoints. This application was developed by a non-expert user during a teacher training. This training was prepared by one of the authors.

4.1. Requirements Analysis Stage

The audience for this application was nursing students (with no specifications regarding age or gender). The students had to know how to navigate the Internet and have the printed marker and a computer with a webcam. The group of teachers listed the requirements, defining the user profile and the functional and non-functional aspects.

Table 2 shows all the requirements listed for this project. In order to obtain a user definition, it was necessary to identify the user's characteristics including gender, education, age, and previous technology knowledge. The non-expert developers defined the functional requirements that would determine the actions executed by the applications, without taking physical constraints into account.

Table 2. Requirements for the epidemiological cycle simulation

User definition	Non-functional requirements	Functional requirements
Nursing students (non-expert users) The students must know how to navigate the Internet	The environment must be illuminated Easy to learn, to understand, and to use The simulation should start immediately when the marker is presented The user can move or rotate the marker to a different position - the simulation should continue Using just one marker to interact with the application because the users are not experts. The application should have animations.	The application should show interactions between mosquitoes and their hosts, (human and non-human primates).

Finally, the developers identified the non-functional aspects, which are requirements that don´t involves users or software directly, for example, the number of markers and the physical environment's characteristics (illumination, physical area, and background).

4.2. Design Stage

Based on the previous information in the Requirements Analysis Stage, the following decisions were made:

- The application would play a mosquito sound during the simulation.
- We chose FLARAS as a software development tool because of the software's simplicity.
- The application must run on the Internet – it does not need to be installed on a hard drive.
- All 3D models were from free repositories.
- Sounds were from a free sound repository.
- The application must be used in an appropriate physical environment, such as a computer laboratory.
- Appropriateness of the physical environment included: ambient lighting, background environment, and the positioning of the user.
- All interactions with the application would be done using a marker.

If this application had been developed by expert users, they could have included a more complex design; for example, they could have incorporated the use of mobile devices and gesture interactions.

4.3. Implementation Stage

The success of this simulation depends on how it interacts with users and how it moves the marker. FLARAS tool allows non-expert users to develop applications. This tool allows the creation of an application that can run on the Internet without programming knowledge. The application was prepared in two weeks during the course.

Figure 7. Epidemiological application.

Figure 7 illustrates how the epidemiological simulation cycle works. It receives an input (interaction from a marker, keyboard, or mouse), processes this interaction (as a rotation or other type of movement) and outputs a real world environment with the addition of virtual objects (3D models and sound).

Figure 8 shows a user interacting with the application using a marker.

Figure 9 shows a user visualizing the objects without the maker.

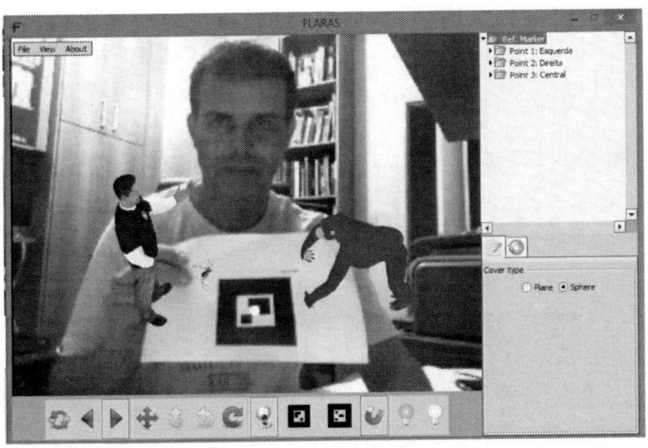

Figure 8. User runs the application using a marker.

Figure 9. User visualizing the application without a marker.

4.4. Test Stage

Although traditional educational methods have proven their efficiency, they also present some deficiencies; for example, they don't promote technologies to illustrate abstract concepts. AR applications, as innovative educational practices, aim to fill this gap, responding to the actual need for change. The evaluation of the epidemiological simulation cycle required verifying its ease-of-use (technical usability) and the application's ability to achieve the learning goal (pedagogical usability). To ensure the pedagogical benefits of these applications, a questionnaire (pre-test/post-test) can be used to measure whether this simulation is increasing, decreasing, or having no effect on student learning. The procedure involves the students filling out a questionnaire prior to and after commencement of the application's use.

Using the work proposed by the non-experts [28], the developers could choose 10 attributes to evaluate the application. Table 3 shows the final questionnaire.

Twenty Nursing students were selected to use and evaluate the application. The developers used a 5-point Likert scale to collect the results. The results are presented in Figure 10.

Table 3. Selected Questions on Martins, Kirner and Kirner [28]

Questions
1. It is easy to handle the marker/object.
2. The response time is appropriate; for example, the images appear briefly on the screen.
3. It is possible to complete the tasks and scenarios quickly using this system.
4. The information is presented in a very organized and easily viewable way.
5. The application presents visual realism.
6. The organization of objects (text, icons, and 3D objects) on the application screens is clear.
7. The animations are well-designed and relevant.
8. Audio aspects of the application are of good quality.
9. It is fun to use.
10. I would recommend it to a friend.

According to Figure 10:

- In general, the application was very well-evaluated: 81% of the users strongly agree with the questions.

- Questions 2 and 5 were better evaluated: 95% of the users strongly agree with the questions.
- While 65% of users strongly agreed with question 6, this is still considered quite positive because the other 35% of users agreed with the question (in other words, none disagreed).

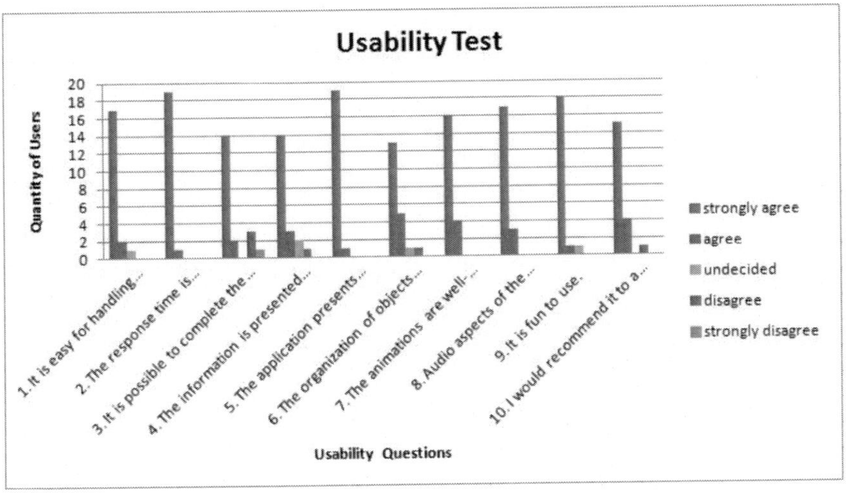

Figure 10. Usability test of the application.

Conclusion

New technologies have supported advances in traditional educational environments and these advances have created new ways for students to learn and for teachers to share knowledge. Augmented reality, one of these new technologies, has been highlighted by the Horizon Report. AR applications allow students to explore objects, perform tasks, learn concepts, and develop skills in an interactive and fun way. By using AR applications in an educational context, each student can explore his or her own interests at his or her own pace. This type of learning is better suited to students' individual characteristics, for example, each student can choose his or her own path of discovery during the navigation of a historical place.

In this chapter, we presented and discussed a development software process by which non-expert users (in this case, teachers) can create AR applications which allow the combination of real images and virtual objects for educational purposes. We expected the teachers to be able to develop their own applications, focusing on the content of the lessons and helping the students to achieve learning goals.

We also showed this process in action during the implementation of an epidemiological application with interaction via a marker, 3D objects, and sound. This AR application was developed by a group of health teachers during a training course. From the observed results, we can conclude that this group can build their own AR applications. However, it is necessary to produce an adequate authoring tool and ensure that virtual objects are available from a repository or built by a support team. A usability test was conducted and the results were very positive.

In future research, we intend to test this process to create new AR applications by non-expert users. We also intend to investigate designing an authoring tool that will assist in the development of applications that can be supported on mobile devices. We also aim to investigate the use of realistic 3D objects that are virtually indistinguishable from a real environment.

REFERENCES

[1] Jones, C., Ramanau, R., Cross, S., & Healing, G. (2010). Net generation or digital natives: is there a distinct new generation entering university?. *Computers & Education*, *54*(3), 722-732.

[2] Hanus, M. D., & Fox, J. (2015). Assessing the effects of gamification in the classroom: A longitudinal study on intrinsic motivation, social comparison, satisfaction, effort, and academic performance. *Computers & Education*, *80*, 152-161.

[3] Kirner, C. (2013). A educação permeando a tecnologia em aplicações educacionais abertas baseadas em hipermídia e realidade aumentada.*Contemporaneidade, Educação e Tecnologia*, *1*(3).

[4] Arvanitis, T. N., Petrou, A., Knight, J. F., Savas, S., Sotiriou, S., Gargalakos, M., & Gialouri, E. (2009). Human factors and qualitative pedagogical evaluation of a mobile augmented reality system for science education used by learners with physical disabilities. *Personal and ubiquitous computing,* 13(3), 243-250.

[5] Wu, H. K., Lee, S. W. Y., Chang, H. Y., & Liang, J. C. (2013). Current status, opportunities and challenges of augmented reality in education. *Computers & Education*, 62, 41-49.

[6] Lee, K. (2012). Augmented reality in education and training. *TechTrends,* 56(2), 13-21.

[7] Azuma, R., Baillot, Y., Behringer, R., Feiner, S., Julier, S., and Macintyre, B. (2001). Recent advances in augmented reality. *Computer Graphics and Applications, IEEE, 21*(6), 34-47.

[8] Kesim, M., & Ozarslan, Y. (2012). Augmented reality in education: current technologies and the potential for education. *Procedia-Social and Behavioral Sciences, 47*, 297-302.

[9] Nincarean, D., Alia, M. B., Halim, N. D. A., & Rahman, M. H. A. (2013). Mobile Augmented Reality: the potential for education. *Procedia-Social and Behavioral Sciences, 103*, 657-664.

[10] Kaufmann, H., & Schmalstieg, D. (2003). Mathematics and geometry education with collaborative augmented reality. *Computers & Graphics,* 27(3), 339-345.

[11] NMC (2012). NMC Horizon Project Short List: 2013 Higher Education Edition, Austin, Texas, The New Media Consortium, 2012. Available: http://www.nmc.org/pdf/2013-horizon-higher-edshortlist.pdf.

[12] Souza, R.C., Moreira, H.D.F., & Kirner, C. (2015). FLARAS 2.0-Flash Augmented Reality Authoring System. Available: <http://ckirner.com /flaras/>. Access: mar. 2015.

[13] Seichter, H., Looser, J., & Billinghurst, M. (2008, September). ComposAR: An intuitive tool for authoring AR applications. In *Proceedings of the 7th IEEE/ACM International Symposium on Mixed and Augmented Reality* (pp. 177-178). IEEE Computer Society.

[14] Kato, H. (1999). ARToolKit. *http://www. hitl. washington. edu/artoolkit/.*

[15] Macintyre, B., Gandy, M., Dow, S., & Bolter, J. D. (2004, October). DART: a toolkit for rapid design exploration of augmented reality experiences. In *Proceedings of the 17th annual ACM symposium on User interface software and technology* (pp. 197-206). ACM.

[16] Grimm, P., Haller, M., Paelke, V., Reinhold, S., Reimann, C., & Zauner, R. (2002). AMIRE-authoring mixed reality. In *Augmented Reality Toolkit, The First IEEE International Workshop* (pp. 2-pp). IEEE.

[17] Di Wu, Y. Y., & Liu, Y. (2009). Collaborative Education UI in Augmented Reality. *ETCS, 9*, 670-673.

[18] Cerqueira, C. S., & Kirner, C. basAR: Ferramenta de Autoria de Realidade Aumentada com Comportamento. In *VIII Workshop de realidade virtual e aumentada. Uberaba–MG–2011.*

[19] Saquosha, "FlarToolKit", 2008, Available: http://saqoo.sh/a/flartoolkit/start-up-guide

[20] Kirner, C. (2011). Prototipagem Rápida de Aplicações Interativas de Realidade Aumentada. Tendências e Técnicas em Realidade Virtual e Aumentada. Porto Alegre, Brasil, 1(1), 29-54.

[21] Sommerville, I. *"Software Engineering"* (2001), 6th ed., Addison Wesley, ISBN 0-201-39815-X.

[22] Pressman, R. S. (2005). *Software engineering: a practitioner's approach*. Palgrave Macmillan.

[23] Sidky, A. S., Sud, R. R., Bhatia, S., & Arthur, J. D. (2002). Problem identification and decomposition within the requirements generation process.

[24] Gause, D.C., & Weinberg, G.M. (1989). Exploring Requirements: Quality Before Design, Dorset House Publishing, New York, 1989.

[25] Maya http://www.autodesk.com.br/products/maya/overview

[26] 3DS MAX - http://www.autodesk.com.br/products/3ds-max/overview

[27] Blender - http://www.blender.org/

[28] Martins, V. F., Kirner, T. G., & Kirner, C. (2015). Subjective Usability Evaluation Criteria of Augmented Reality Applications. 17th International Conference on Human-Computer Interaction. In *press*.

[29] Breakwell, G., & Millward, L. (1995) *"Basic Evaluation Methods"*, BPS Books, Leicester

In: Augmented Reality
Editor: Raymond Hughes

ISBN: 978-1-63482-902-1

Chapter 2

CONTRIBUTION OF AUGMENTED REALITY TO MUSICAL EDUCATION AND MUSIC THERAPY

***Valéria Farinazzo Martins**[*]*
***and Ana Grasielle Dionísio Corrêa**[†]*
[1]Faculdade de Computação e Informática,
Universidade Presbiteriana Mackenzie, Brazil

ABSTRACT

This chapter aims to discuss the use of augmented reality (AR) applications to the area of music education and music therapy. Three applications will be presented that have been developed by the authors, tested by experts in music education and children in schooling process (Music-AR), and music therapist and children with Cerebral Palsy in Music Therapy (GenVirtual and MusicandoRA). It is a multidisciplinary research involving different professionals: engineers, computer scientists, musicians, therapists and educators. In addition to the scientific contributions generated in this work, deserves its technological contribution, given that the three applications are available for free use.

[*] valeria.farinazzo@mackenzie.br.
[†] ana.correa@mackenzie.br.

1. INTRODUCTION

According to Azuma and Billinghurst [1], Augmented Reality (AR) is a technology that enables the user to see the real world, with virtual objects superimposed upon or composited with the real world. AR system has the following three characteristics: combines real and virtual, it is interactive in real time and it is registered in 3D.

AR was originated from another technology called Virtual Reality (VR). While VR can be defined as an advanced interface to computer applications, where the user can navigate and interact in real time in a 3D synthesized environment, using multisensory devices. AR simplifies its use because a non–conventional device is not required, just a webcam and markers are necessary [2]. Although it emerged in the 60s, only 30 years later it started being used in various fields of knowledge and educational applications.

AR was indicated by the Horizon Report [3] as one of the technologies that will revolutionize education in the next coming years. This is due to their fun and interactive features, among other reasons. The possibility of using AR education applications is made possible by: cheapening and improvement of the hardware and the need for more user-friendly interfaces for interaction with non-expert users; and the indispensability to work with other ways of teaching, using active practices. In this sense, using computers in the classroom allows, in many cases, simulation of situations not previously possible or imagined. According to Schafer [4], musical education should be directed to all and not only to those who demonstrate an aptitude. The author deals with the musical teaching as a creative process, but still little practiced in traditional teaching.

In health, AR feature provides access for people with physical disabilities to virtual environments facilitating educational and therapeutic procedures [5]. AR allows leveraging the processing of conventional rehabilitation through motivation: the patients presented themselves motivated to perform the exercises in a different way which allowed them to be out of the routine of conventional exercises [5, 6].

The union of these both areas (Augmented Reality and Music) can find several potential applications that are not being extensively explored. It is possible, for example, to use the playful nature of Augmented Reality applications to motivate the teaching of music perception in schools [7, 8] or to use it in music therapy area [5, 9].

The importance of using AR for musical perception teaching comes from the fact of Musical Education again become mandatory content in Brazilian schools (Law No. 11,769 of August 18, 2008). Thus, one should investigate the use of emerging technologies in the musical teaching-learning process.

On the other hand, the use of AR in music therapy reaches its importance because it becomes more a motivating resource for working methods of music therapy (improvisation, recreation and music composition, sound and musical imitation) [5]. AR allows perform repetitive exercises more attractive with visual and auditory representations that motivate the patient, to obtain objective measures of exercise (speed of limbs, range of motion, hit rates and/or error scores in games, among others) and to increase or reduce the complexity of the exercises, according to the planning of the music therapist [9]. Furthermore, with AR is possible create different computer systems for users unable to use conventional device such as keyboard and mouse [9]. AR can facilitate the interaction of individuals with severe motor problems. The handling of virtual objects can occur naturally, dragging or touching an object with fingers or hands, without necessarily using adapters to interact [5, 9].

However, there are only few studies in the literature that address the use of AR in the field of arts; specifically in musical education, it becomes even more scarce [10, 11, 12], as well as in music therapy [5, 9].

This chapter aims to discuss the use of AR applications to the area of music education. Three applications will be presented that have been developed by the authors, tested by experts in music education and children in schooling process (Music-AR) and children with Cerebral Palsy in Music Therapy (GenVirtual and MusicandoRA). It is a multidisciplinary research involving different professionals: engineers, computer scientists, musicians and educators. In addition to the scientific contributions generated in this work, deserves its technological contribution, given that the three applications are available for free use.

The work is structured as follows: Section 2 "Augmented Reality and Music Education and Music Therapy" presents the main concepts essential for understanding the subsequent sections as well as the related work involving music and augmented reality for education and therapy. Section III presents the software “Music-AR”, “GenVirtual” and “MusicandoRA”. Section IV presents the instructions for use of our software and use of results of reports conducted with children in schooling and children with Cerebral Palsy. Finally, in Section VI, “Conclusions”, a discussion on the benefits of music augmented reality software can bring to support the process of music education and music therapy is presented.

2. Augmented Reality in Music Education and Music Therapy

This section presents the important topics for the understanding of the work. Thus, the following subsection presents the main concepts of musical education and music therapy. Subsequently, we present the main works related in the literature.

2.1. Musical Education

According to Schafer [4], music is an organization of sounds (rhythm, intensity, melody and timbre), with the intention of being heard. In this regard, the vision of musical art transcends the orthodox definitions of classical, popular and folk music and personal preference. Therefore, music can also be described as an imitation of nature or daily sounds.

According to the author [4], the awareness of environmental sounds occurs through much training. The musical education provides training people to be able to preserve familiar sounds and create new ones. Thus, it should listen to, analyze and make sounds. Still, for the author, musical education should be constantly linked to the experiences and discovery, just so you can get efficient results. These experiences and discoveries should happen very early in childhood.

Therefore, in order to understand music, people must be able to distinguish the meaning of sound properties [4, 13]:

- Pitch: refers to the bass, midrange and treble, i.e., how high or low a sound is.
- Timbre: sound quality that distinguishes instruments. It is the personality of the sound.
- Intensity: It is the strength which the sound occurs.
- Amplitude: It is the variation of sound intensity.
- Melody: the sound movement by difference frequency.
- Duration: It is the variation of sound time; its extremes are: long and short.

Music should elicit different emotional responses in listeners, which are generated because they assume that the different extremes related to these aforementioned sound characteristics (e.g., high and low, strong and smooth, short and long, fast and slow) must have some power over emotions. This can be used to create a composition with a specific character that may affect the listeners' emotional state. [13, 14].

2.2. Music Therapy

Music therapy is the use of music and its elements (sound, rhythm, melody and harmony) by a qualified professional in a patient or group in music therapy process to facilitate and promote communication, respect, learning, mobilization, expression and other goals therapeutic relevant to achieve physical, emotional, mental, social and cognitive [15]. The music therapy aims to develop potential or establish the individual functions so can achieve better intra and / or interpersonal integration and, consequently, a better quality of life through the prevention and rehabilitation [16].

The music therapy process can develop according to various approaches and methods, the most common being [15]: improvisation, recreation and music composition, sound and music listening and musical imitation. The goal is to develop potential and / or restore functions of the individual to achieve a better quality of life through prevention, rehabilitation or treatment.

The pleasure and fun provided by the music can increase the yield of physical rehabilitation sessions, while regular exercise become repetitive and tiresome. The music therapy activities can provide distraction from pain, discomfort and anxiety, which can often be associated with physical disability [17].

Activities involving the performance of musical instruments can improve the range of motion movement (fine or thick). The use of percussion instruments, when positioned around the individual, can provide body stability and arouse the interest of the individual to the use of the upper limbs [18]. The coordination of the fingers can be improved through the use of musical instruments that require greater precision in fine motor movement [18; 19].

Recently the largest successful and recognised applications in the music therapy area has been the treatment of chronic pain and post-traumatic stress [20; 21].

2.3. Related Work

Traditional music education often places a great emphasis on individual practice. Studies have shown that individual musical practice is often not very productive due to low motivation and interest of students [22]. System fosters should promote interest and motivation, as this will increase practice time and hence, most likely, learning outcomes. Thus, AR has been identified as a suitable technology for the above goals, due to its ability to create a perceptual and cognitive overlap between instrument (keys), instructions (notes), and music (sound).

Chow et al. [22] used AR to create a perceptual and cognitive overlap between instrument and instructions to stimulate development in notation literacy and to create motivation through presenting as a game the task that was perceived as a chore. The user wears the head mounted display and sits in front of the keyboard. The keyboard connects to the computer using a MIDI interface. The video captured by the cameras in front of the device is projected onto the display to create the AR effect. The representation of musical notes in the system indicates visually in which key each written note corresponds to. The text and music are synchronised using visual cues. Each note is represented as a line above the corresponding key, where the length of the line represents the duration of the note. The notes approach the keys in the AR view in a steady time. When the note reaches the keyboard, the corresponding key should be pressed. Similarly, when the end of the note reaches the keyboard, the key should be released.

Huang et al. [23] presents another work about AR based piano teaching system, which tracks the real keyboard of piano naturally. Following the virtual hands augmented on the keyboard, beginners of piano can practice playing piano. Instead of the marker in traditional AR system, the geometrical parameters of the piano keyboard are detected to create a marker. We first extract all the contours of the image, from which possible contours of keyboard are found. This way, the keyboard area is identified by the structure of white and black keys predefined. The authors evaluated the system with speed and accuracy.

Klebber et al. [24] conducted an experiment using AR to learn a guitar musical instrument. The guitar system uses LED lights embedded in the fretboard to give direct information to the guitarist as where to place his/her fingers. This was compared to a standard scale diagram. Results indicate that this system led to initial significant gains in performance over a control condition using diagrams.

Many other studies present positive results from the use of AR for learning musical instruments as: piano [25], guitar [26] and percussion [27].

Many music therapists use music technology in their clinical work [28]. Despite the great potential of augmented reality to music therapy, there are few studies on this area in the literature. So far, augmented reality has been used as an attractive tool to support the process of learning music, but no major concerns with the interaction of people with disabilities with music.

In addition to the work undertaken with the GenVirtual and MusicandoRA treated in this chapter, it was found only one work that uses AR in music therapy: Francisco et al [28] created an AR application that uses music and visual therapy. It is an alternative tool for managing the mental stress level of an individual. The developed system enables the users to relax and unwind anywhere at any time. The goal of the software is to reduce the user stress level through audio and visual presentation alongside with the integration of augmentation of the original setting and application of appropriate concepts from music and visual therapy, with a web camera support.

Given the benefits provided by this technology in relation to the forms of interaction, we assume that the music therapist procedures when directed to people with disabilities can be facilitated by the use of this technology. In addition, systems designed with augmented reality can be easily accessed at home, which can enhance the treatment, including possibilities for remote monitoring. Another relevant factor is the potential of this technology to improve motivation and satisfaction of patients and positively influence their treatment in rehabilitation. In this research we describe the GenVirtual and MusicandoRA to support music therapy and its evaluations.

3. Augmented Reality Musical Software

3.1. Music-AR

The first work presented in this chapter is about an application called "Music-AR". It was designed based on interviews with a teaching music expert, Arts Coordinator of a private teaching school located in the city of São Paulo, Brazil. Information gathered through this interview has shown shortages of software for teaching children musical perception. According to the interviewed, few software only teach the trivial, such as musical notes. It is necessary, however, teaching sound properties that precede musical teaching, such as pitch, rhythm and timbre. Thus, the goal was not to teach music or a musical instrument, the core focus was to develop an application that can teach musical perception in children.

Flaras[1] [29] tool was used for developing the application. Although you can import 3D objects ready, for reasons of ease and adequacy of the objects they were created. As the target audience were children, Music-AR should have the following requirements: be attractive, playful, easy to use, easy to learn, fun, intuitive and visually pleasing. The development took about a month and involved two developers, authors of this work.

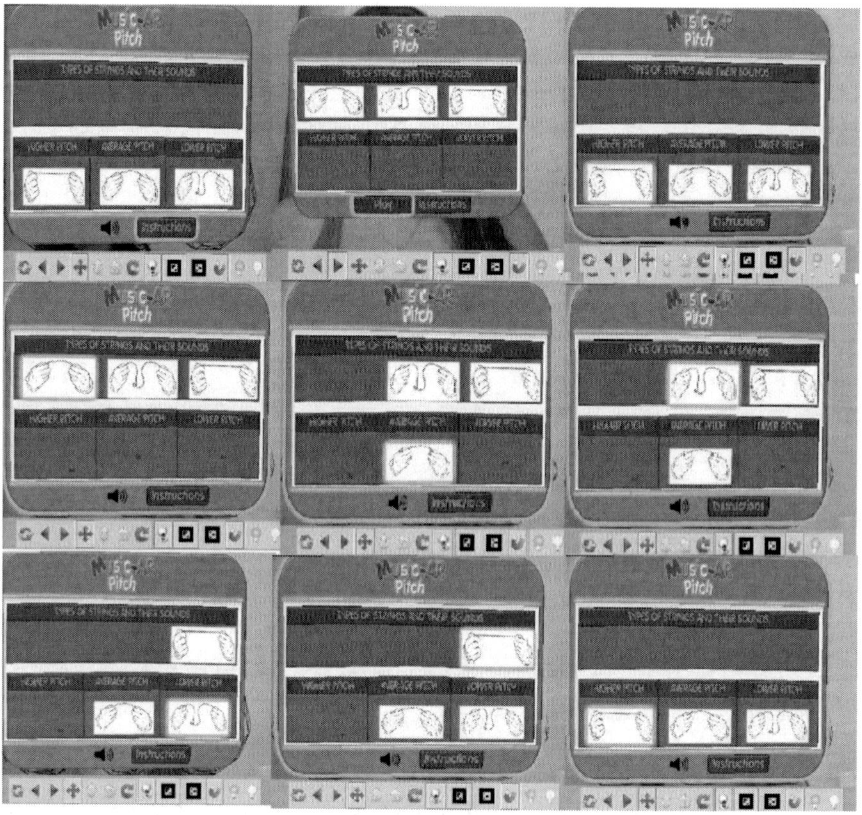

Figure 1. Main screens running the game on the Pitch.

[1] Flaras is a authoring tool, with free open source software available on the Internet at a site. It has support material, including: downloadable versions of the tool; tutorials based on texts and videos; faq; e-book; repository with various online applications, accompanied by their respective projects open, licensed to adaptation and creation of derivative works; and information about its developers.

To achieve these goals, short and intuitive games (exercises) were generated. All games allowed the child to hear / see explanations about it and then use the concepts learned to solve the exercises. This application was divided into four little games. The first is about “pitch”. To explain the concept of pitch, the application brings the idea to stretch and loosen a rope - respectively high and low; this is what really happens in the stringed musical instrument. Figure 1 shows the sequence that the user performs one of the games - regarding the topic "Pitch".

The second game is about “Sound Intensity”. This concept is relate to the strength with which the sound occurs In this exercise, the child after hearing an explanation about "Sound Intensity". Three bees buzzing are presented, giving the feeling of distance - the closest or farthest bee - and the sound with greater or lesser intensity. Figure 2 shows the main screen for the application of sound intensity.

Figure 2. Main screens running the game on the Intensity.

The third game is about "Duration" concept. In this case, the child should listen to the explanations of short and long sounds (the variation of sound time). Afterwards, the child should hear a certain sound and decide if it is long or short. A screen with feedback on the correctness or error is shown to the child. Figure 3 shows the main screens for the application of "Duration".

Figure 3. Main screens running the game on the Duration.

Finally, the last game is related to the concept of timbre. This concept is related to the personality of the sound; it is the ability to separate two sounds of different instruments, such as the sound of a piano and the sound of a violin. After listening to the explanations about timbre, the child must decide which sound is listening to. A screen with feedback is shown to the child. Figure 6 presents the main screen for the application of "Timbre".

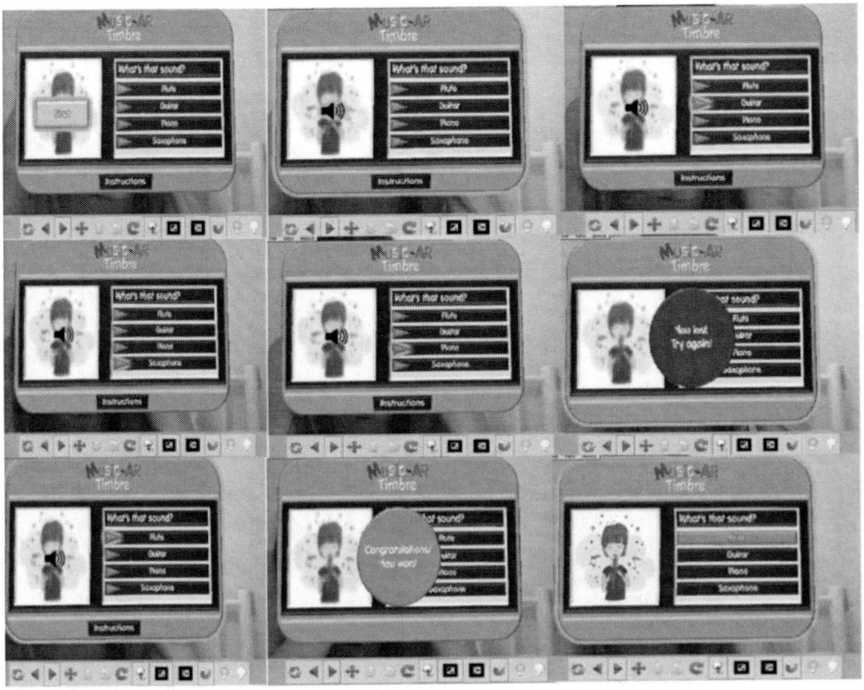

Figure 4. Main screens running the game on the Timbre.

3.2. GenVirtual

GenVirtual is an augmented reality musical environment that allows developing creation activities, improvisation and musical reproduction such as composition and reproduction of melodies, listening to musical sounds, and musical memory games.

GenVirtual allows adding to the real world, three-dimensional virtual elements (colored cubes) capable of simulating sounds of several musical instruments like wind instruments, strings and percussion. Sounds are executed playing the virtual elements with hands, without use of conventional interaction devices (mouse, keyboard, joystick) and adapters for individuals with low mobility.

Identification of markers (cards) on table happens through the processing of images, captured by a webcam, connected to a computer, strategically positioned on the superior part of the table (Figure 5). Symbol card is detected and associated to a sound. The emblem of a piano is the standard sound associated to cards, but there is the possibility to change the emblem of musical notes emitted by cards. For this, it is enough to add a new marker on the table containing the desired musical instrument. In this way, the same virtual elements emit different sounds, according to instrument defined by new card. It could assume emblems of wind instruments (flute, trombone, trumpet, etc.) or string instruments (violin, guitar, etc). Another possibility is to use cards with symbols corresponding to percussion instruments, as drums, tambourines, triangles, as well as symbols that represent sounds of electronic instruments.

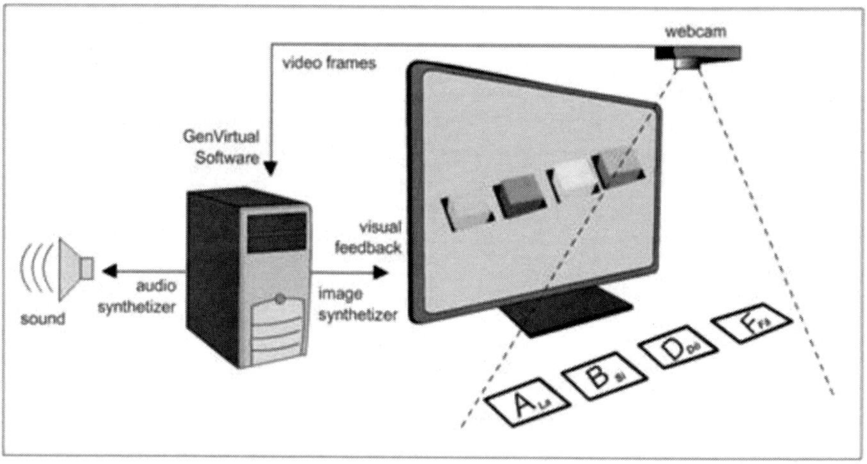

Figure 5. GenVirtual Interface.

The differential in this music system is the flexibility of cards for interaction. The cards can be printed in different colors and proportions, allowing the therapist to perform a unique motor planning for each individual, in accordance with the desired motor challenge. The cards can be organized in different ways on the table, or on the floor, where the interaction takes place. Figure 6 shows GenVirtual use in a patient with motor disabilities.

GenVirtual also has a game called "follow sound-and-colors" (Figure 7), that makes it possible to stimulate the attention, concentration and memorization of colors and sounds. In this case, GenVirtual generates a musical sequence. The virtual cubes rotate in agreement with the musical sequence to be played, and simultaneously, the musical note regarding that virtual cube is executed. The musical notes are emitted one per time, and the system is awaiting the user's interaction that should obstruct the marker regarding the emitted musical note. To each success, the sequence wins a new item (musical note), increasing the challenge of memory and retention of information game.

Figure 6. Rehabilitation with GenVirtual.

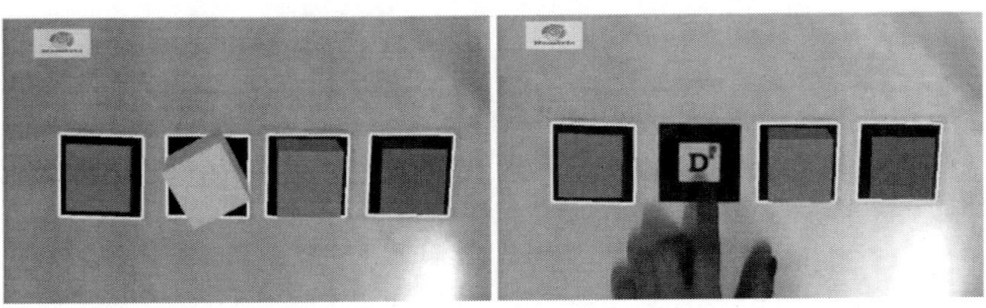

Figure 7. Memory Game of the GenVirtual.

Experiments with GenVirtual were performed in music therapy intervention. The GenVirtual, the use of information and a brief report of the use of the tool in music therapy sessions in patients with Cerebral Palsy are presented in the next section.

3.3. MusicandoRA

MusicandoRA is an Augmented Reality software accompanied by a book of music theory. Among the topics musical content in the book include: the sound and silence, the difference between the bass and the acute sound, musical notes, musical instruments, rhythms, among others. Each of these contents has one or more interactive activity with Augmented Reality. For example, when the subject is musical instruments, in addition to the explanatory text, it can view the instrument in 3D, through augmented reality software (Figure 8). For this, the user must put the reference marker, which is the book's page on the webcam's field of vision. In this example, the 3D image of a guitar appears on screen superimposed on the book marker.

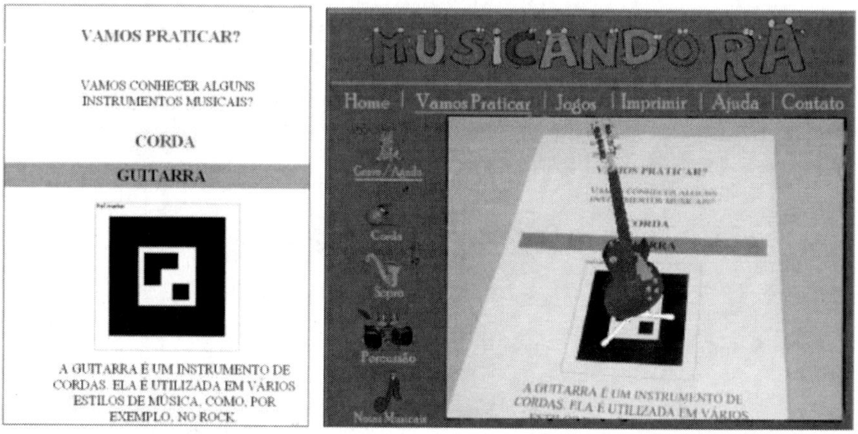

Figure 8. Book and software MusicandoRA.

MusicandoRA book has two interaction boards: one to start audio or animation (Figure 9a) and another to pause the execution of audio or animation (Figure 9b).

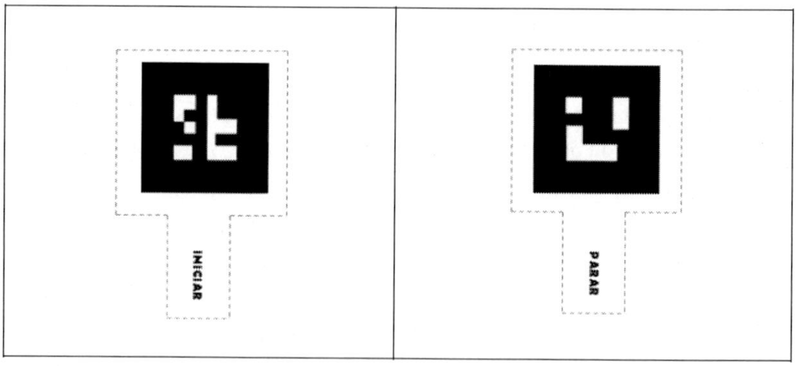

Figure 9. (a) Board to start; (b) Board to pause.

When placing the plate in the webcam view, the guitar melody audio will run. Thus, the user can enjoy the guitar melody at the same time he visualizes the instrument in 3D. When rotating the book on the webcam's field of vision, it is possible see the guitar in various perspectives (front view, side view and rear view).

Several string, wind and percussion instruments are treated in the book and all have interactive activity augmented reality. Just as in the activity with the guitar, it is possible to view the 3D musical instruments and enjoy its melodies (Figure 10).

Figure 10. (a) Guitar; (b) Trumpet (c) Drums.

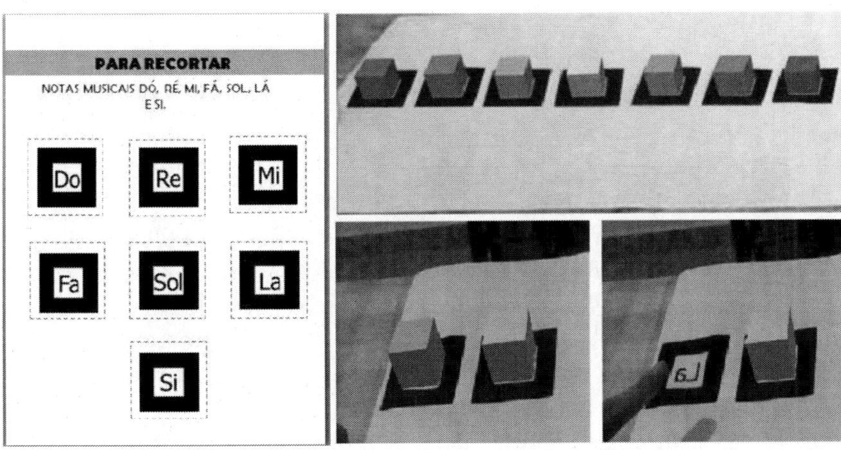

Figure 11. (a) interactive activity augmented reality with musical notes.

The musical notes (C; D; E; F; G; A; B), are presented in MusicandoRA book as signals which represent the tone pitch of the sound. In this activity, the color representation was adopted to differentiate high and low sounds: warm colors for acute sounds and cool colors for bass sound. Therefore, we have: C (purple blue); D (blue); E (green); F (pink); G (yellow); A (orange); B (red). The user can crop the reference markers, printed in the book page and then spread them in the scene (Figure 11). Each marker represents one of the musical notes, and to be positioned in front of the webcam, produces a colorful 3D cube. When approaching finger on one of the markers, the sound of the corresponding musical note is played on the piano timbre.

Bass and acute sounds can be also worked with other visual representations. In another activity, the bass sound is represented by an animal that has the deep voice, the lion (Figure 12), while to represent an acute sound, we use the image of a bird (Figure 12). Both 3D images have an animation that can be triggered with the interaction of board start. The animation shows the bird whistling and lion roaring.

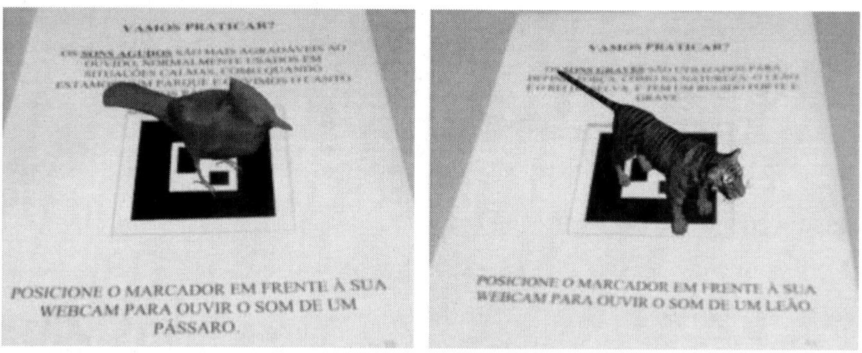

Figure 12. (a) bird singing; (b) Lion roaring.

MusicandoRA has various musical challenges to be solved at the end of the book. One challenge is to try to identify the corresponding musical instrument with the melody that is running. First the software loads the images of two musical instruments (Figure 13a). Then it performs a part of a melody. From this, the user must touch the corresponding reference marker to the musical instrument which relates the tone of that melody. If this is correct, MusicandoRA software issues hit message and performs the complete song (Figure 13b). In the case of error, the software issues an error message and prompts the user to try solving the challenge again (Figure 13c).

The challenge becomes more difficult to solve as the user progresses the difficulty levels. In the first level the user have to choose between two musical instruments only. The third level has three instruments and so on. Until reach the last level showing five musical instruments simultaneously.

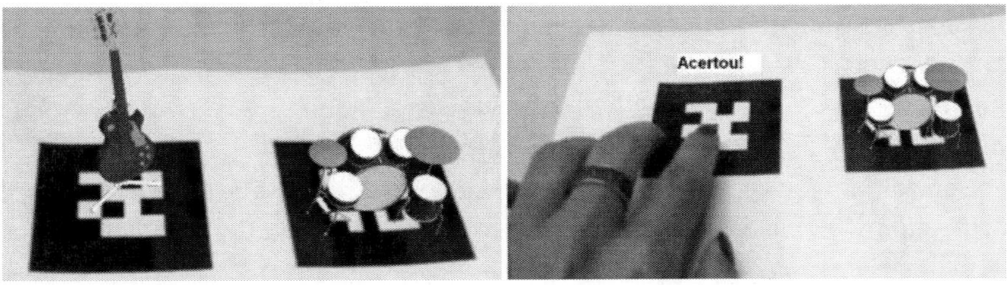

Figure 14. (a) Musical Instruments challenge; (b) Correct; (c) Error.

The second challenge consists of a musical band and the user should try to find what musical instrument that is not a part of the musical band. This challenge is more complex than the first, because the user needs to perceive the sounds of all the instruments that are run by the musical band. The complexity increases according to the amount of instruments that make up the musical band: the first level is raffle, a song with only two instruments; on the second level the band has three instruments and so on until the user reach the seventh level, where the band performs musical instruments.

4. Indicators to Use the Tools

This section presents the instructions for the use of our software and use of results of reports conducted with children in schooling and children with Cerebral Palsy

4.1. Music Education

The music education is the process of construction of musical knowledge, whose main objective is to awaken and develop a love for music, stimulating and contributing to the overall formation of the individual. The music education is done through play activities for the development and improvement of auditory perception, imagination, coordination, memory, socialization, expression, spatial perception, etc. The playful works as motivator and encouragement for the development of musical expression where imitation, perception and creation are the main elements of this process.

Music-AR was developed for children from pre-school, aged between four and six years old. Its use should complement classroom learning music in school or private classes, teaching concepts that are earlier than teaching a musical instrument, that is, music perception education. Thus, through regular classes and the use of games, children should learn the sound characteristics: pitch, intensity, duration and timbre. It is not address to be used without monitoring by an adult.

In order to validate Music-AR games, we developed two types of evaluation which were performed: tests with potential end users and evaluation with a music teacher.

For tests with potential end users, a group of 14 children of both genders (nine girls and five boys) was selected. The age of the children varied among five and seven years old. Five children had had contact with AR. Eight children had had contact with musical education.

By observation techniques, it could note some difficulty in the use of the software which is related to problems of usability of the technology itself, such as those caused by inadequate light or lack of detection of the marker in a few moments. On the other hand, all the children could understand the musical perception using the applications.

About the usability questions, all the children answered that they believed the layout of four applications as appropriate and attractive; that they liked the sounds of the applications and also the use of them and would like to use this type of technology frequently. On the other hand, by an interview with a music teacher, the following results were obtained:

- The teacher did not know the technology of RA, but considered it important to be used for music education.
- The teacher considered the applications are very interesting and fun and that could really help in teaching music.
- The teacher believes that these games are easy to manipulate and that kids would not have a problem with it.

She considered that more games should be developed and then organized into a kit and distributed to children.

4.2. Music Therapy

GenVirtual indications beyond the scope of rehabilitative therapy, allow household use of the system. With systematic and repetitive use of GenVirtual, individuals are spontaneously motivated. This can be enhanced with memory cognitive rehabilitation and visual stimuli (colors of virtual objects), as well as audio stimulation (sound of virtual objects). Therefore, motor rehabilitation is exercised with repetition of the sequence of motor movements necessary to strike the sounds. Some activities of the MusicandoRA can be also used in memory cognitive rehabilitation and visual stimuli through, for example, of colored cubes that reproduce the sounds of musical notes. The difference is that the GenVirtual has a larger library of musical timbre while the MusicandoRa is limited to the piano timbre. The MusicandoRA can be used through a web page. The GenVirtual, by contrast, must be installed on computer and runs without the Internet.

From the analysis of music therapy approaches, Bunt and Stige [15] establishes the four main methods of music therapy: improvisation, re-creation, composition and listening. All these methods can be applied using GenVirtual and MusicandoRA. For the clinical cases, the re-creation method was used, where the patient performs, reproduces, transforms or interprets a piece of music or musical model as a whole. The objectives of clinical re-creation, according to Bunt and Stige [15] can be:

- Develop sensory motor skills.
- Promote rhythmic behavior and adaptation;
- Improve care and guidance;
- Develop memory;
- Promote the identification and empathy with others;
- Develop skills of interpretation and communication of ideas and feelings;
- Learn to play specific roles in various interpersonal situations.

We can consider that music therapist intervention with an individual with an extremely hypotonic hand, for example, can be processed by GenVirtual in the following aspects: these individuals are not able to keep their fingers extended on the keyboard, or do not have the enough muscular strength to strike piano keys or strum a guitar [9].

Typically, in these cases, the patient uses adaptations like tips on the hands to play the piano, tambourine fasteners for bimanual hand use, and the help of a music therapist to carry out interventions of music expression, the "music making" [9]. With GenVirtual and MsicandoRA, the performer can use his/her hands closed into a fist to play a musical note, since the cards can be printed in larger proportions. There is no need to adjust the interaction with the virtual environment. To use GenVirtual to play an instrument, the user needs to cover a card without using adaptations.

Experiments with GenVirtual were made with children with Cerebral Palsy in sessions of music therapy. The plan to use GenVirtual in this situation was:

- Extension of arm exercises: the goal is to achieve a virtual object. Due to flexibility of the cards, it's possible to create the desired motor challenge for each patient according to their unique motor limitations;
- Flexion exercises in the wrist: support forearm on the table and bend the wrist up and down, playing virtual objects to execute sounds;
- Repetitive motor training: sequence of motor movements facilitated by the game's musical memory;
- Visual perception exercises: identify musical elements from the representation of these elements by color virtual objects;
- Auditory perception exercises: identify bass and treble sounds (listen sound) and identify known melodies (music listening);
- Reproduction and development of more sophisticated music: experiencing the "music-making" aimed at expanding their cognitive functions such as attention, concentration and memory.

The results of this research, still preliminary, showed that GenVirtual can serve therapeutic interventions including learning of cognitive, motor, psychological, social, and to stimulate musicality. The music therapist made a plan of possible activities to be developed with the use of this system in their interventions. Since it is based on conventional computing platform, this system can already be used in home environment. This may provide family's involvement in complementary activities.

CONCLUSION

This chapter presented a discussion about the use of Augmented Reality applications to the area of music education and music Therapy. Three applications that have been developed by the authors, were presented: Music-AR, MusicandoRA and GenVirtual. It is a multidisciplinary research involving different professionals: engineers, computer scientists, musicians and educators. In the first application presented, Music-AR, it was possible to present the use of AR for teaching musical perception in Brazilian children, especially on pitch, sound intensity, duration and timbre.

By the observation results, it is possible conclude that children could understand, through using Augmented Reality, the concepts of pitch, sound intensity, duration and timbre - sound properties that must be learned before teaching music. All children could solve the musical perception exercises. Augmented Reality seems to be adequate for use with children, due to its playful nature technology. Augmented Reality can be used as a tool in the learning-teaching process of musical perception.

Flaras is a very easy tool to be used by non-specialist people. On the other hand, it is a little limited, exactly by the same point. Some types of exercises on musical perception could not be performed due to lack of resources in the tool. For example, it´s impossible include a selection command (if-then and if-then-else). This command is used by programmers to determine what will happen if a certain event occurs. In the case of the "if" statement, if a certain event is true, then the command will be executed.

In the second and third application, GenVirtual and MusicandoRA, can be useful to include therapeutic interventions for cognitive learning, motor, psychological and social stimulation through musicality. Reviews with them were made with children with cerebral palsy and proved the effectiveness of the interface for those with reduced mobility and that usually require adjustments in conventional computer interface for interaction.

In addition to assisting in the training of motor coordination, both GenVirtual as MusicandoRA can help: the learning of musical symbols; creation and / or reproduction of published or known melodies, as both software enable interaction with musical notes; the "music-making"; planning and reproduction of more sophisticated musical pieces expanding the cognitive functions such as attention, concentration and memory. Despite these potential in education, the use of GenVirtual and MusicandoRA in teaching and music learning process have yet to be investigated. It is intended, therefore, to evaluate these two software in musical initiation classes with children and experts.

Social programs have disseminated computers even in low-income families. And since the system is based on a conventional computational platform, the prototype can already be used at home. This may provide family involvement in complementary activities. Therefore, the sequences of operations with GenVirtual may involve stages of maturation or development, gradual learning, development of personal relationships, the performance, composition and spontaneous child improvisation, exploration, experimentation and alternatives selection, as well as ongoing evaluation of the effects of therapy on patient's progress through treatment targets.

Nevertheless, the virtual environments do not replace conventional medical therapies, but the tool will help empower existing treatments.

References

[1] Azuma, R., Baillot, Y., Behringer, R., Feiner, S., Julier, S., And Macintyre, B. (2001). Recent advances in augmented reality. *Computer Graphics and Applications, IEEE*, 21(6), 34-47.

[2] Kirner, C. and Kirner, T. G. (2007). Virtual reality and augmented reality applied to simulation visualization. In *Simulation and Modeling: Current Technologies and Applications*, 1, 391-419.

[3] NMC (2012). NMC Horizon Project Short List: 2013 Higher Education Edition, Austin, Texas, *The New Media Consortium,* 2012. Available: http://www.nmc.org/pdf/2013-horizon-higher-edshortlist.pdf.

[4] Schafer, R. M. (1993). *The soundscape: Our sonic environment and the tuning of the world.* Inner Traditions/Bear & Co.

[5] Correa, A.G.; Assis, G.A.; Ficheman, I. K.; Lopes, R.D.; Nascimento, M. (2014). Perception of Health Professional about Clinical Utility of an Augmented Reality Musical System to Motor and Cognitive Rehabilitation In: *XVI Symposium on Virtual and Augmented* Reality (SVR), 71 – 79.

[6] Assis, G. A.; Correa, A. G. D.; Martins, M. B. R.; Pedrozo, W.G.; Lopes, R.D. (2014). An augmented reality system for upper-limb post-stroke motor rehabilitation: a feasibility study. *Disability and Rehabilitation: Assistive Technology,* v. 1, 1-8.

[7] Gomes, L.; Martins, V.F.; Colombo, D.D.; Paiva, M.G. (2014). Music-AR: Augmented Reality in Teaching the Concept of Sound Loudness to Children in Pre-School. In: *XVI Symposium on Virtual and Augmented Reality* (SVR), 114 – 117.

[8] Gomes, L.; Martins, V. F.; Puzzelo, V. R. (2013) Music-AR: Software for teaching children music perception. In: *9th Iberian Conference on Information Systems and Technologies (CISTI),* June, Barcelona, 1-6.

[9] Correa, A.G.D.; Ficheman, I. K.; Nascimento, M.. Lopes, R.D. (2012). Contributions of an Augmented Reality Musical System for the

Stimulation of Motor Skills in Music Therapy Sessions. *Learning Disabilities.* 1ed.Rijeka Croácia: In-Tech, v. 1, 275-288.

[10] Chow, J., Feng, H., Amor, R. And Wünsche, B. C. (2013). Music education using augmented reality with a head mounted display. In *Proceedings of the Fourteenth Australasian User Interface Conference-*Volume 139 (pp. 73-79). Australian Computer Society, Inc.

[11] Huang, F., Zhou, Y., Yu, Y., Wang, Z. and DU, S. (2011). Piano ar: A markerless augmented reality based piano teaching system. In Intelligent Human-Machine Systems and Cybernetics (IHMSC), *2011 International Conference on* (Vol. 2, pp. 47-52). *IEEE.*

[12] Keebler, J. R., Wiltshire, T. J., Smith, D. C. and FIORE, S. M. (2013). Picking up STEAM: educational implications for teaching with an augmented reality guitar learning system. In *Virtual, Augmented and Mixed Reality. Systems and* Applications (pp. 170-178). Springer Berlin Heidelberg.

[13] Zatorre, R. J. (1984). *Musical perception and cerebral function: a critical review*. Music Perception, 196-221.

[14] Wiggins, J. (2001). *Teaching for musical understanding.* McGraw Hill.

[15] Bunt, L.; Stige, B. (2014). *Music Therapy: An art beyond words.* Routledge: second edition.

[16] Rice, R.R.; Johnson, S.B.; A Collaborative Approach to Music Therapy Practice in Sensorimotor Rehabilitation (2013). *Music Therapy Perspective,* Oxford Journals, v.3, n.1, 58-66.

[17] Yeo, J. H.; Cho, D. Y.; Oh, M.M.; Park, S.S.; Park, M.G. (2013). *Journal of Endourology.* v.27, n.4, 459-462

[18] Thaut, M. H.; Macintoch, G. C.; Hoemberg, V. (2015). Neurobiological foundations of neurologic music therapy: rhythmic entrainment and the motor system. *Front. Psychol,* v.5, n. 1185, 1-6.

[19] Altenmüller, E.; Schlaug, G. (2013). Neurologic music therapy: The beneficial effects of music making on neurorehabilitation. *Acoustical Sciense and Technology,* v. 34, n. 1, 5-12.

[20] Gutgsell, K. J.; Schluchter, M.; Margevicius, S.; Degolia, P.A.; Maclaughlin, B.; Harris, M.; Wiencek, C. (2013). *Journal of Pain and Symptom Management,* v. 48, n. 6, 822-831.

[21] Carr, C.; Ardenne, P.; Sloboda, A.; Scott, C.; Eang, D.; Priebe, S. (2012). Group music therapy for patients with persistent post-traumatic stress disorder – an exploratory randomized controlled trial with mixed methods evaluation. *Psychology and Psychotherapy: Theory, Research and Practice,* v. 85, n.2, 179–202.

[22] Chow, J., Feng, H., Amor, R. And Wünsche, B. C. (2013). Music education using augmented reality with a head mounted display. In *Proceedings of the Fourteenth Australasian User Interface Conference-* Volume 139 (pp. 73-79). Australian Computer Society, Inc.

[23] Huang, F., Zhou, Y., Yu, Y., Wang, Z. And Du, S. (2011). Piano ar: A markerless augmented reality based piano teaching system. In Intelligent Human-Machine Systems and Cybernetics (IHMSC), *2011 International Conference* on (Vol. 2, pp. 47-52). *IEEE.*

[24] Keebler, J. R., Wiltshire, T. J., Smith, D. C. and Fiore, S. M. (2013). Picking up STEAM: educational implications for teaching with an augmented reality guitar learning system. In Virtual, *Augmented and Mixed Reality. Systems and Applications* (pp. 170-178). Springer Berlin Heidelberg.

[25] Shah, K. N., Rathod, K. R. and Agravat, S. J. (2014). A survey on Human Computer Interaction Mechanism Using Finger Tracking. *International Journal of Computer Trends and Technology,* v.7, n. 3.

[26] Shiino, H., De Sorbier, F. and Saito, H. (2013). Towards an augmented reality system for violin learning support. In Advances in Depth Image Analysis and Applications (pp. 136-145). Springer Berlin Heidelberg.

[27] Yamabe, T., and Nakajima, T. (2013). Playful training with augmented reality games: case studies towards reality-oriented system design. *Multimedia Tools and Applications,* 62(1), 259-286.

[28] Hahna, N.D.; Hadley, S.; Miller, V.H.; Bonaventura, M. (2012). Music technology usage in music therapy: A survey of practice. *The Arts in Psychotherapy,* v. 39, n.5, 456–464.

[29] Francisco, J., Comendador, B. E., Concepcion Jr, A., Tapao, R. and Dalluay, V. L. (2013). VisuaLax: Visually Relaxing Augmented Reality Application Using Music and Visual Therapy. In *International Proceedings of Economics Development & Research,* 63.

[30] Souza, R.C.; Moreira, H.D.F.; Kirner, C. (2015). FLARAS 2.0-Flash Augmented Reality Authoring System. Available: <http://ckirner. com/flaras/>. Access: mar. 2015.

In: Augmented Reality
Editor: Raymond Hughes

ISBN: 978-1-63482-902-1

Chapter 3

A MULTI-VIEW MARKERLESS AUGMENTED REALITY ENVIRONMENT FOR MEDICAL DATA VISUALIZATION

Márcio C. F. Macedo[1]*, *Caio S. B. Almeida*[1]†, *Antonio C. S. Souza*[1]‡, *Antonio L. Apolinário Jr.*[1]§ and *Gilson A. Giraldi*[2]¶
[1]Federal University of Bahia (UFBA), Brazil
[2]National Laboratory for Scientific Computing (LNCC), Brazil

Keywords: geometric algorithms, languages and systems, three-dimensional graphics and realism, augmented and virtual realities

ACM Computing Classification: I.3.5, I.3.7., H.5.1.

Abstract

On-patient medical data visualization is desirable in several practical situations such as surgical planning and medical training. Currently,

*marciocfmacedo@gmail.com
†caiosba@gmail.com
‡antoniocarlos@ifba.edu.br
§apolinario@dcc.ufba.br
¶gilson@lncc.br

it becomes possible with the augmented reality, a technology which enables the visualization of patient virtual anatomy at the location of the real one in a conventional display. In this chapter, we present a multi-view marker-free augmented reality environment for on-patient medical data visualization which supports: volume rendering, advanced methods for real and virtual data composition, rigid and non-rigid tracking and additional features such as occlusion. To achieve real-time performance, the most critical algorithms take advantage from the graphics processing unit to reduce processing time. Moreover, the multi-view architecture of the application includes an augmented reality glasses and two RGB-D sensors, one to capture the observer (i.e., physician) and the other to capture the observed structure (i.e., patient region of interest). The results obtained from an evaluation of the proposed environment highlight that it runs in real-time and provides good visual quality for the final augmented scene.

1. Introduction

Physicians see medical data, typically patient's anatomical structures, on a monitor and they must analyze and mentally compose what is shown on the screen to the patient. This mental model of the patient's anatomy will serve as basis for health care in routine examinations or time-critical situations. Therefore, the physicians must have sufficient knowledge over patient's and general human's anatomy to proceed appropriately during any operation (e.g., diagnosis, surgery). In this context, we investigate how to provide better visualization of patient's relevant information such that physicians may be able to perform a medical procedure properly.

With the availability of the Augmented Reality (AR) technology, one can take over this task of mental mapping by transferring it to a computer. Specifically, we can provide on-patient or *in-situ* medical data visualization in order to allow the physician to visualize, at the same time, the patient and a part of his anatomy. The solutions in this area can be used for surgical planning, training, medical diagnosis and post-operative examination.

Augmented Reality is a technology in which the view of a real scene is augmented with additional virtual information. Medical AR is a sub-field of AR in which the virtual entity is a medical data. In an ideal scenario, a successful medical AR environment must support the following requirements:

1. Real-Time Performance - In the field of computer graphics, an application is considered to be in real-time if it runs equal or above 15 frames per second [1]. This concept is more related to user interactivity, because when the user interacts with the application the feedback must be received quickly.

2. Accurate Tracking - By registering two surfaces or textures captured at previous and current frames of the scene, the current camera pose can be estimated. Therefore, the virtual object can be positioned and tracked into the augmented scene, giving the illusion that it coexists at the same location in the real world;

3. Volume Rendering - When the virtual entity consists of a 3D medical data, it requires a special attention to the way it will be rendered. Volume rendering is a field which is concerned with techniques for generating images for this kind of data, therefore being necessary for a medical AR application;

4. High Visual Quality - To improve user's perception of the augmented scene, real and virtual medical data must be rendered according to simple methods such as superimposition and blending or advanced methods such as focus + context visualization, depending on the medical AR application;

Due to the popularity of freely available AR libraries, such as ARToolkit [2], ARTag [3], FLARToolKit [4] and FLARAS [5], the creation of AR applications which use fiducial markers for tracking of the virtual object became easier. However, in medical AR, fiducial markers can be intrusive in the scene and uncomfortable, mainly when the target model is the patient's body. Moreover, in general, they do not give support for non-rigid tracking of the virtual data due to the rigid nature of the registration method [2–5], although some alternative techniques have already been proposed to overcome such problem [6–8].

Another distinction between general AR and medical AR is related to the type of virtual data. Most of the AR applications use polygonal models for rendering. However, volumetric models are commonly used for rendering in medical AR due to the popularity of 3D scanners based on computed tomography (CT) and magnetic resonance imaging (MRI) data for medical procedures.

Regarding the experience, AR can be classified in two different ways depending on how the user sees the mixed world. When the user sees the mixed world pointing his eyes directly to the real positions of the object or scene, this experience is classified as *direct view*, while when the user sees the mixed world through a monitor screen or projector, this experience is classified as *indirect view* [9]. From the viewpoint of medical applications, it is not natural for the user (being it a physician or not) to be looking at the merged scenario via the screen of his personal computer. Therefore, AR glasses can be used in order to guarantee a *direct view* experience to the observer. Besides, multi-view solutions based on AR glasses, Head-Mounted Displays (HMD) or portable solutions based on mobile devices can be employed to allow a more seamlessly visualization of the virtual content onto the real scene [10].

To improve the visual understanding of the scene by the physician, it is fundamental for a medical AR application to provide high quality rendering of the virtual objects to be combined with the real scene. One solution for this issue is to show patient's anatomic region of interest not as an isolated object, as done conventionally, but in the context of the patient's body. This not-so-new solution, formally known as focus + context (F+C) visualization paradigm, has been studied and developed since many centuries ago [11]. As already stated by Bichlmeier and colleagues in [12], Leonardo da Vinci (in 1510) and Vesalius (in 1543) have already proposed the use of F+C visualization to understand the disposition of inner organs, bones, muscles and blood vessels in the context of the human body. So, based on this paradigm, the physician may understand the relative positioning of patient's anatomy (focus region) while visualizing patient's body (context region) [12].

Hence, an AR environment for on-patient medical data visualization should take into consideration these additional features (i.e., markerless tracking, multi-view visualization, volume rendering and F+C visualization) still running in real-time on customer hardware.

In this chapter we present a multi-view markerless AR environment for on-patient medical data visualization with support to F+C visualization and non-rigid tracking of the real scene. An overview of the main components and their relationships is illustrated in Figure 1. Markerless augmented reality (MAR) tracking is achieved by generating a 3D reference model of the patient's region of interest (ROI) and tracking it during the live stream. On the other hand, 3D

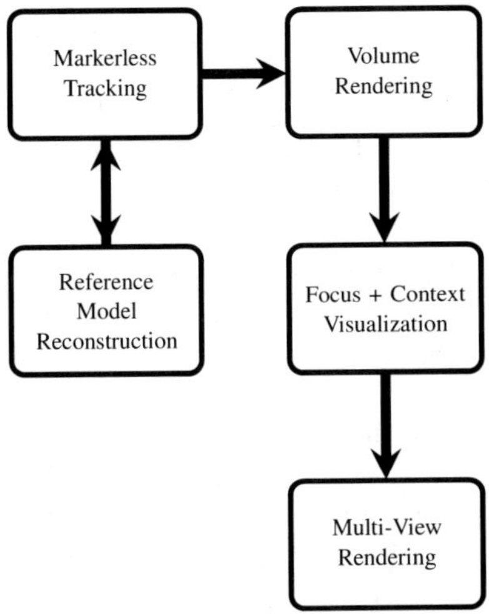

Figure 1. Integrated solution for multi-view markerless on-patient medical data visualization viewed as components and their relationships.

reference model reconstruction requires markerless tracking to align the different viewpoints acquired from patient's ROI. Non-rigid support for tracking is added by using a three-level adaptive solution which updates the 3D reference model based on the current deformation estimated. From the estimated camera pose, medical volume can be rendered and displayed to a physician inside patient's anatomy at the location of the real one. Volumetric medical data is rendered according to standard volume rendering techniques. After volume rendering, F+C visualization techniques are used to define which parts of the volume will be visualized in the final augmented scene. For the final visualization, a multi-view solution based on two RGB-D sensors and AR glasses is employed to allow the seamlessly visualization of the virtual content. Real-time performance is achieved by implementing rigid, non-rigid markerless tracking and 3D reference model reconstruction on the Graphics Processing Unit (GPU). Moreover, to improve user's perception of the augmented scene, the application supports occlusion.

The remaining of this chapter is organized as follows. Section 2 provides a review on recent related works on AR and on-patient medical data visualization. Section 3 introduces the multi-view infrastructure of our approach. Section 4 presents the MAR environment. Section 5 is dedicated to present how to achieve non-rigid tracking in this environment. Section 6 discusses the tests conducted and the experimental results. In Section 7, the conclusion regarding the present work is presented.

2. Related Work

2.1. Augmented Reality

Augmented Reality is a field of Computer Science in which the user's view of a real scene is augmented with additional virtual information. Since this concept has become popular by the seminal works of Ronald Azuma and colleagues [9, 13, 14], many researches have been conducted focusing on how to solve the problem of accurate and real-time tracking, which is one of the main technical challenges of AR.

In the end of 90s, the main method to position a virtual object and track a real scene in real-time relies on the use of an artificial fiducial marker. The squared shape of the marker allows its fast recognition and tracking, while the symbol inside it is used as an marker ID, which identifies the virtual object that must be rendered. Due to the simplicity of this approach, libraries like ARToolKit [2], ARToolKitPlus [15] and FLARToolKit [4] are still used to help on the creation of AR applications, even using the traditional fiducial marker as basis for tracking [16–18].

With the advance in terms of computational resources for customer hardware, many techniques have been proposed to allow the use of any object visible in the scene as a natural marker. In these cases, tracking is based on the selection of keypoints (e.g., pixels with high curvature or localized on corners) or edges extracted from the color image. A survey on this subject can be found in [19].

For marker-based AR, tracking must operate only on the image space, according to the features of the pixels. The main drawback for this color or texture-based tracking are the susceptibility to illumination conditions and marker occlusion, which may affect the accuracy of the tracking algorithm. To overcome these problems, depth-based tracking algorithms have been proposed [20]. As such algorithms are based on the depth of the scene instead of its color, they are robust to the variation of illumination conditions, however still suffering from the problem of occlusion.

Due to the high performance and accuracy of the existing depth-based tracking algorithms, the use of fiducial markers for positioning of the virtual object and tracking of the real scene is no longer essential for AR applications. Hence, AR can be markerless, where a part of the real scene is used as natural marker instead of using an artificial fiducial marker. In this scenario, tracking becomes more complex, since there are no markers in the original scene. Markerless AR is desirable in several situations such as the ones for on-patient medical data visualization. The algorithm most used for depth-based tracking is the real-time variant of the Iterative Closest Point (ICP) algorithm [20], which has already GPU implementation [21].

In our MAR environment, we use a markerless tracking algorithm based on the reconstruction of a 3D reference model which represents our natural marker. Accuracy and robustness for tracking are improved by using a pose estimation algorithm [22–24].

2.2. Non-Rigid Tracking

Markerless AR uses geometric information of part of the real scene as a natural marker. By using it as a point of reference for tracking, one can expect non-rigid motion of the natural marker if it consists of a deformable object (e.g., face, body, hand).

Differently from the rigid tracking, which is widely used in AR due to its simplicity and real-time performance, non-rigid tracking requires more attention. It faces the same issues from rigid registration and also the problem of deformation, which itself increases the number of parameters to be estimated and the space of solutions that can be found. Unlike the rigid scenario, where every point (or pixel, in 2D) from a given source object must be moved by a single transformation measured by the algorithm, in the non-rigid scenario, every point may undergo a different, interconnected deformation.

One of the first works in the field of fast non-rigid registration applied to computer graphics was the Embedded Deformation (ED), a real-time deformation algorithm for object manipulation and creation of 3D animation [25]. The goal of this technique is to allow an user intuitive surface editing while preserving surface's features. Deformation, in this case, is represented by a graph. Each node of this graph is associated with an affine transformation that influences the deformation to the nearby space. The great advantage of this approach is that it can be applied to a wide range of objects, articulated or not.

Although its main goal is the user object manipulation, the ED algorithm also can be seen as a non-rigid registration algorithm in which source and target surfaces are the object's geometry before and after a non-rigid motion. In this sense, many researchers have used or improved this approach to the specific problem of non-rigid surface registration, focusing on improving the accuracy of the original approach [26–29]. In general, these methods require execution time in the order of minutes to register two point clouds. Thus, they are not suitable for AR applications.

Few methods were capable to achieve real-time performance in depth-based non-rigid registration. Chen et al. proposed a method for non-rigid registration of skeletons captured from user's body [30]. Their approach runs in 30 frames per second (FPS) but uses a small number of constraints for registration and depends on a skeleton definition.

Nutti et al. proposed a method to track tumors based on patient's body position that presumes the prior knowledge about the scenario [31]. Their algorithm runs in 10 FPS.

Zollhofer et al. proposed a method for real-time non-rigid registration of arbitrary meshes captured from the real scene [32]. Based on a hardware specialized for high-quality surface acquisition, their approach generates a 3D template model of the object of interest and uses a hierarchical non-rigid registration algorithm fully implemented on the GPU. The implementation runs in 30 FPS with high accuracy.

In our multi-view markerless AR environment for on-patient medical data visualization environment, we use the non-rigid tracking approach proposed in [33]. Like [32], our approach is also based on the ED algorithm, does not require prior knowledge of the object and takes advantage from GPU parallelism to achieve real-time performance. However, no special hardware is supposed to be used. On the contrary, our approach is based on a simple off-the-shelf depth sensor, with noise and low accuracy. We use an adaptive graph refinement to improve non-rigid registration accuracy. Differently from other approaches, our algorithm runs entirely on the GPU and is based on a quadtree which operates over the 2D projection of the object to be registered [34].

2.3. On-Patient Medical Data Visualization

Medical AR systems for on-patient medical data visualization have been driven by different approaches in recent years. Kutter et al. proposed a marker-based method for real-time on-patient visualization of volume data on a Head Mounted Display (HMD) [35]. Their work focuses on efficient implementations for high quality volume rendering in an AR environment. They also provide occlusion handling for physician hands. An improved version of this work was proposed by Wieczorek et al. to handle with occlusions due to medical instruments as well [36]. Also, they included additional effects in the system, such as virtual mirror and multi-planar reformations.

Lee et al. proposed a registration framework for a medical AR system [37]. They used three cameras: two of them mounted to form a stereo vision system and reconstruct patient's head; the other camera used to capture the images of the patient in real-time. In a pre-processing step, a surface is reconstructed from CT and a variant of the ICP algorithm is used to do the image-to-patient registration. The estimation of the third camera pose is done by using a fiducial marker.

In the field of anatomic education, Blum et al. proposed the *mirracle*, a magic mirror for teaching anatomy [38]. They used a display device and a Kinect sensor to allow volume visualization of a CT dataset augmented onto the user. To track user's pose, a skeleton tracking algorithm was employed. As the system was initially designed for educational purposes, they could use a generic CT volume which was scaled to the size of the user and augmented onto him. Some authors have proposed a direct extension to this work, improving the accuracy of the positioning and tracking of the medical data [39] or directing it for other applications, such as the ones for bone anatomy learning [40].

Mercier-Ganady et al. presented a novel MAR application for on-patient brain activity visualization [41]. User's head is tracked by using a face tracking algorithm native from Microsoft Kinect SDK. Brain activity is computed from an electroencephalography cap (EEG), which is worn by the user.

Kilgus et al. proposed a mobile MAR environment for on-patient medical data visualization to support forensic pathologists during autopsy [42]. A structured light sensor is mounted on a mobile device, similarly as done in previous work [43], and it is used to capture color and depth sensor of the body being analyzed. These data are sent to a server which estimates the current camera pose, projecting the color information of the medical data at the body's position.

The approaches proposed in [35–37] share the same drawback: they use markers to help in the calibration, positioning and tracking of the objects in the scene. The use of fiducial markers provides fast and accurate tracking. However, these markers are still intrusive, because they are not part of the original scene. Moreover, the hardware of the optical tracking system in some applications is too expensive. The approaches that do not use such marker-based hardware, in general, do not obtain real-time performance in its application due to the computational cost of the markerless tracking in conjunction with the volume rendering techniques used, which require additional processing time in comparison with polygonal model rendering. One exception for this situation is the *mirracle* system and its extensions/improvements. Nevertheless, the main drawback of the skeleton tracking used is that it does not track accurately some parts of the body, such as head. Another exception is the approach proposed for brain activity visualization [41] which uses a specific technique for face tracking.

The approach we proposed in our environment for on-patient medical data visualization is based on markerless tracking and it runs entirely in real-time with low-cost hardware components [44–47]. Moreover, in terms of visual quality, we integrate into our approach the main techniques proposed in this field, such as Contextual Anatomic Mimesis [12] and Context-Preserving Volume Rendering [48, 49], to enhance the augmented visualization of the virtual internal structures on the patient, instead of just superimposing the virtual content on the scene.

3. Multi-View Markerless Infrastructure

The multi-view augmented reality environment used in this work is based on the one proposed by Almeida [50, 51]. As long as our target scenario is a medical AR system, we build a infrastructure based on two main components: an observer (physician) and a target model (patient). The Figure 2 pictures its main components.

- Observer - He is the user of the system that wears a pair of augmented reality glasses and is positioned in front of the target model (which can be a human being, for example, or a static object). On a medical context, the observer would be a medical specialist that observes the patient and analyses the combination of the real image (part of the patient body) with a virtual image (from magnetic resonance imaging or computed tomography). The observer is able to move his head.

- Augmented reality glasses - The augmented reality glasses are worn by the observer and have two cameras. The images captured from the target model will be merged with virtual images and displayed on the two lenses of these glasses. On one of the approaches implemented by this work, the observer motion is determined from sensors present on the glasses: accelerometers, magnetometer and gyroscopes. Based on sensor data, it is possible to determine the variation on the orientation of the glasses, and so it is possible to know how much the observer has moved his head. This calculation returns values that define motion on longitudinal axis, vertical axis and lateral axis. The virtual image should be re-projected in real time according to those movements.

- Target model - The target model (a human being, for example), is placed in front of the observer and does not use any kind of fiducial marker. The main goal is that the target model can be tracked in real time even without any marker. In order to calculate where and how the virtual image should be displayed, it is necessary to identify the position and orientation of the real object relative to the observer. This is done based on two Kinect sensors placed on the environment.

- Sensors - Two RGB-D sensors are placed on the environment, where the first one captures geometric data from the observer and the second one captures geometric data from the target model. The information captured by the sensor directed to the target model is used to reconstruct a 3D reference model of his region of interest, which is used for tracking and can be merged with a virtual image (Section 4.1.).

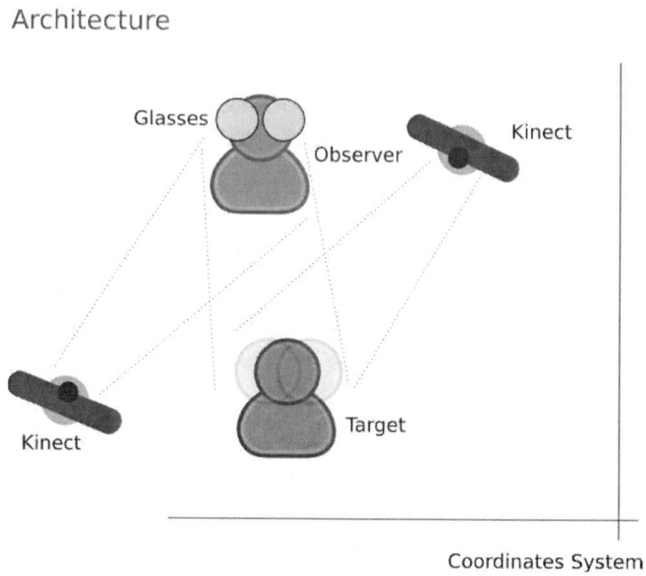

Figure 2. Global view of the multi-view environment

In this framework, the observer and target model are positioned one in front of the other, with some restriction of minimum and maximum distance. The observer can see the composition of a real image with a pre-defined virtual image over the target model, through the augmented reality glasses (alignment - be able to track where to place the virtual image - is a fundamental goal in this process). The observer and target model can move themselves around their own axes, in a way that the virtual image adapts itself in real time to fit the new viewing angles. Everything is performed without fiducial markers.

Each device (glasses and sensors) presented on this multi-view environment has its own coordinate system, but all information must be converted to a global one. Since there are two sensors and one pair of augmented reality glasses, we need to implement two different approaches: one that uses the augmented reality glasses to determine the observer's pose (based on data from accelerometers and magnetometer) and another one that uses a second Kinect device to determine the observer's pose based on a reconstruction of his model. On Figure 3 it is described the pipeline for the multi-view augmented reality application designed

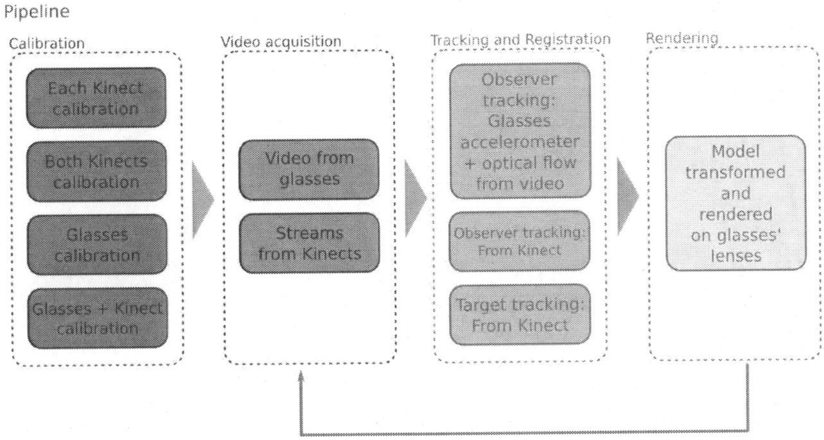

Figure 3. Augmented reality pipeline

on this work.

On the calibration stage, it is necessary to execute the following tasks: (a) Calibrate each Kinect device separately; (b) Choose one Kinect sensor and calibrate it with respect to the other one; (c) Calibrate the AR glasses; (d) Calibrate the glasses with respect to the Kinect that captures the target model. On the video acquisition stage, the environment gets video streams and depth streams from both RGB cameras of each Kinect as well as the video stream from the glasses' lenses. On the tracking and registration stage, there are different approaches for tracking the observer (by just using the glasses or by using a second Kinect), while the target model is always tracked by a Kinect device. Information from the Kinects are registered as point clouds while information from the glasses are registered as transformation matrices. Finally, the target model, transformed to the observer's viewing point, is rendered along with some virtual image and displayed on the glasses' lenses. The diagram at Figure 4 represents the main components of the augmented reality environment and their main features.

Once observer and target are aligned on a common reference system, they can be tracked, which will be explained on the following section.

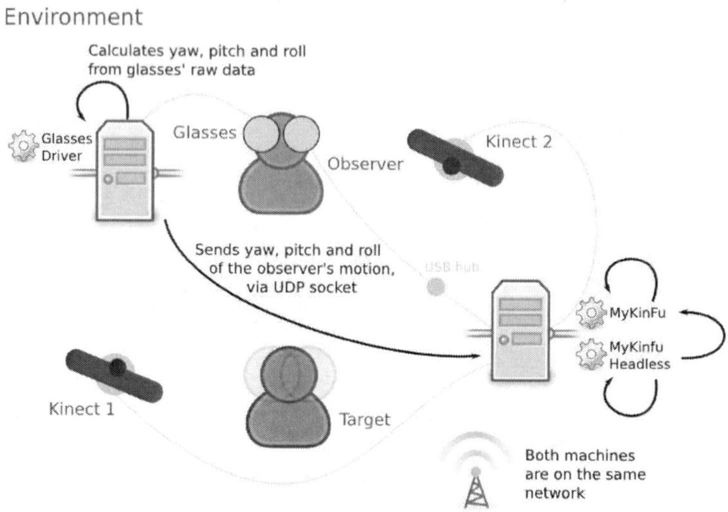

Figure 4. High level representation of the augmented reality environment implementation

4. Markerless Augmented Reality Environment

4.1. Markerless Tracking

For markerless tracking, we used the solution proposed in [44] which is depicted in Figure 5. The proposed approach requires an RGB-D sensor (i.e., a sensor which provides color and depth data) and a computer with GPU, hardware components present in the multi-view environment shown in Section 3.. We have chosen to use the MS Kinect [52] as RGB-D sensor to capture patient's color and depth information. Real-time performance is achieved by using parallel processing power of the GPU in all critical algorithms.

After capturing color and depth data, we segment the natural marker (e.g., patient's ROI) from the scene by applying the Viola-Jones face detector implemented in GPU to locate and segment the face in color image (Figure 5) [53]. By assuming that depth and color cameras are calibrated (Section 3.), we can easily map the segmented location from color to depth image.

The Kinect sensor is known to provide noisy depth data. To deal with this issue, the depth map is denoised by using a bilateral filter [54]. Next, the depth of the background scene is segmented by applying a depth threshold on the filtered depth map. The filtered depth map then can be converted into vertex and normal maps for every input frame.

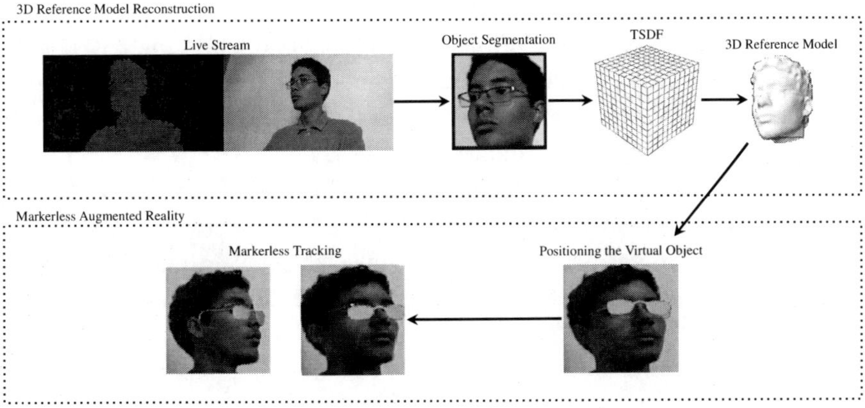

Figure 5. Overview of the proposed markerless tracking solution.

With the natural marker properly segmented, we need to track it through the RGB-D sensor live stream. To do so, we integrate the different viewpoints acquired from the scene into a single reference model (Figure 5) and use this model as basis for registration, in order to improve tracking accuracy [21].

KinectFusion algorithm is used in this context to reconstruct a 3D reference model of the object of interest in real-time [21]. This algorithm integrates raw depth data coming from a depth sensor into a 3D grid to produce high-quality 3D reconstruction of a scene. The grid stores at each voxel the distance to the closest surface (i.e., Signed Distance Function - SDF) [55] and a weight that indicates uncertainty of the surface measurement. For a single view, SDF values are positive in-front of the surface, negative behind and zero-crossing where the sign changes. In KinectFusion, SDF is only stored in a narrow region around the surface, which means that just a truncated SDF (TSDF) is stored. Surface extraction is achieved by detecting zero-crossings through a ray caster.

3D reference model reconstruction is done only on the 3D reconstruction stage and is the basis for MAR live tracking. The reconstruction is stopped by the user and the virtual data can be positioned (Figure 5.)

After virtual data positioning, MAR live tracking is started (Figure 5). In fact, live tracking is done in two steps: during reconstruction of the 3D reference model and during MAR with the user and the virtual data. For real-time rigid tracking, we use the real-time variant of the ICP algorithm [20]. As already mentioned, the use of the 3D reference model by the ICP allows a more consistent rigid registration with less incremental error [21]. After the rigid transformation estimation, it is applied to the virtual data, which can be composed with the real scene captured by the Kinect.

One problem of the real-time variant of the ICP algorithm is that it uses the projective data association to find correspondences between the objects we want to register. Basically, in this association, each point is transformed into camera coordinate space, projected into image coordinates through a perspective projection and the corresponding points are that on the same image coordinates. The ICP fails (i.e., does not converge to a correct registration) when there is not a small pose variation between sequential frames. For improving the tracking robustness, we take advantage that our ROI is the patient's head and we use a head pose estimation algorithm to give a new initial guess to the ICP for correctly computation of the current transformation [22]. As we propose the use of this approach in an AR environment, we have used the real-time head pose estimation described in [56].

The proposed MAR solution supports occlusion by using the depth maps of the current (captured by the depth sensor) and previous (represented by the 3D reference model) frames. Where the current depth data is in front of the previous one, the volume is the occludee (i.e., occluded). Otherwise, it is the occluder.

4.2. Integration of the Markerless Tracking in the Multi-View Infrastructure

Two different approaches were tried for allowing markerless tracking in the multi-view environment. The first one is based on a Kinect that captures the target model and on a pair of augmented reality glasses, worn by the observer, that also sees the target model but has a tracker that provides information about the glasses' rotation. The translation on this approach comes from an optical flow feature, based on Lucas-Kanade algorithm [57], that tracks feature points from the glasses' video as identified by the Shi-Tomasi [58] algorithm applied on the video frame. A composition of the rotation with the translation gives the final rigid transformation from the observer that can be used to track the target model and keep it aligned with what the observer sees.

The second approach is based on two Kinects. One of them is still employed for the same purpose as on the first method: it tracks and reconstructs the target model. The second Kinect is placed on the opposite direction and captures the observer. Based on the transformations suffered by the observer's model due to the actual observer's motion, it tracks the target model and keeps it aligned with the image captured by the glasses' camera.

4.3. Non-Rigid Tracking

Although markerless rigid tracking works well for several scenarios, when the natural marker (patient's ROI) is deformed, the algorithm is unable to track such deformation and may fail. In this case, if an algorithm for relocalization [68,69] is not used or if the deformation still occurs in the sequential frames, probably the application must be restarted. To enable real-time non-rigid tracking of the patient's ROI, we use an adaptive non-rigid registration algorithm [33], whose overview is illustrated in Figure 6.

After object detection and segmentation, points from the source (P_s) and the target (P_t) surfaces are associated by using the projective data association [20]. Next, inspired by the ED model [25], our algorithm builds a deformation graph (G) on P_s to allow its deformation to P_t iteratively. Each node $g \in G$ consists of a point in P_s associated with a 3D affine rigid transformation (i.e., a 3D rotation matrix R and a 3D translation vector t) which influences the deformation to the nearby space. To select the nodes of G, a quadtree is built on GPU to perform the selection of nodes based on the 2D projection of G. As the nodes of G are also points in P_s, we can convert them from world to image coordinates by using the same process used to reproject P_s into depth map.

P_s may be an object with holes distributed along the surface. In this case, the selection of nodes only based on the 2D space may cause the nodes to be selected in regions where there is no depth data. To solve this problem, we take advantage from what we call virtual nodes to represent the space where there is no depth data. Virtual nodes favor the expansion of the quadtree in regions

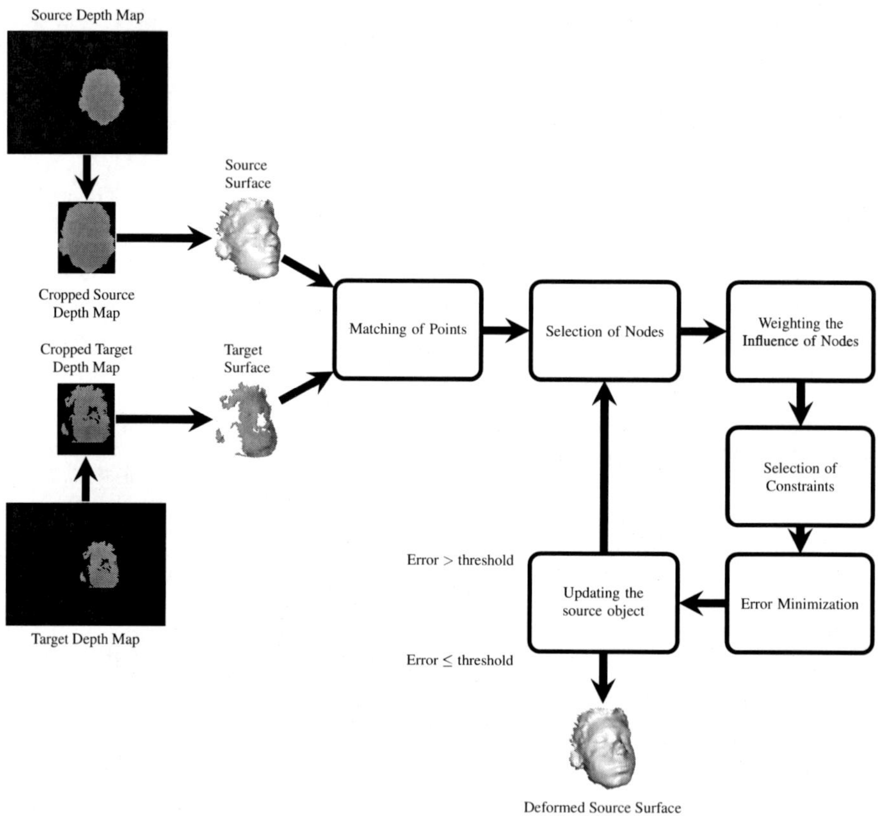

Figure 6. Overview of the proposed non-rigid registration algorithm from the depth map acquisition to the final non-rigid aligned surface.

where naturally we have depth data, however not in the specific position of the node. It is worthy to mention that virtual nodes do not have affine transformation, they are just leaves of the quadtree that can be refined to generate real leaf nodes if necessary. Therefore, we use virtual nodes only in the first two levels of the quadtree.

The algorithm for node selection can be divided in two steps: the building of the quadtree and the adaptive refinement/collapse of nodes in G.

We build the quadtree in the first iteration of our algorithm. The GPU kernel that selects the nodes is called iteratively from the first level to the level required by the user to build the quadtree. Each GPU thread, in parallel, is uniformly assigned to a position on the 2D projection of P_s to select a node. In the first level, if the point assigned to the GPU thread is visible, then, it will be a new node in G. In the opposite case, it can be a new virtual node. On the next levels, if the node is selected, the GPU thread removes the parent node from G and inserts it into a parent list.

For collapsing of nodes, the GPU kernel is iteratively called from the last to the first level of the quadtree in order to collapse the nodes in a bottom-up fashion. Each GPU thread, in parallel, is assigned to a node in G. Then, the GPU thread checks if the node has children and if it is at the current level that is being iterated. If the thread passes from these conditions, given a region C around the 2D position of the node, it computes the average of an energy function (defined in [25]) for each point $\in C$. If the average energy is below a certain threshold, the children nodes in C must be collapsed. To collapse the nodes, a thread checks if exists child nodes and if they are leaf nodes. In this case, they are collapsed and the region C is represented by the old parent node.

For refinement of nodes, the GPU kernel is iteratively called from the first to the last non-empty level of the quadtree in order to refine the nodes in a top-down fashion. Each GPU thread, in parallel, is assigned to a node in G. Then, the GPU thread computes the average error around a region C. If the average is above a pre-defined threshold, the node must be refined. After the refinement (i.e., creation of four new child nodes), the GPU thread removes the parent node from G and inserts it into a parent list.

Once the node selection is completed, the influence of the k-nearest nodes for each point of P_s is computed. Formally, a point p can be deformed by G according to the following equation:

$$p' = \sum_{j=1}^{k} w_j(p)[R_j(p - g_j) + g_j + t_j] \tag{1}$$

where k represents the k-nearest nodes of p, R_j is 3D affine rigid transformation, g_j is the j-nearest node, and w_j is a weight that measures the influence of each node to the point. The normalized weight w_j can be computed as follows:

$$w_j(p) = (1 - ||p - g_j||/dist_{max})^2, \tag{2}$$

where $dist_{max}$ is the distance to the $k+1$-nearest node with respect to p.

From the Equation 2, it is guaranteed that the nearest nodes will have more influence in the deformation of p. Also, as the nodes are points of P_s, they are deformed by other nodes of G.

To efficiently compute the weights in GPU, we create an array that contains only the nodes selected. By using this array, we have direct access to the nodes of G, removing the need to check explicitly on the surface whether a point is also a node. Then, each GPU thread computes the influence for a specific node in G.

Instead of using all the points from P_s as constraint for the optimization or asking the user to perform this task of constraint selection, we employ an adaptive algorithm that performs the selection of constraints based on the residual error previously measured. Given a region on P_s, the higher the error, the higher the number of points selected as constraints for the optimization.

In the first iteration, where the residual error still was not measured, an uniform sampling is used to select the constraints. To do that, a $n \times n$ mask, with step n, is scanned through the 2D projection of P_s at the xy coordinates. The point at the center of this mask is selected to be a constraint if it exists in P_s (i.e., it is not in a hole). From empirical tests, $n = 4$ produced the best results.

In the remaining iterations, we use the same $n \times n$ mask to perform a scan on the 2D projection of P_s and its residual error. First, the algorithm evaluates the average residual error at the $n \times n$ region being scanned. Based on the average error E_{avg} and a pre-defined threshold th_c, the number of points selected at that region will be defined. In this case, we consider three situations:

- $E_{avg} > th_c$, all the n^2 points are selected;
- $E_{avg} >= th_c/2$ and $E_{avg} <= th_c$, n points uniformly distributed over the mask are selected;
- $E_{avg} < th_c/2$, only the point at the center of the mask is selected;

Therefore, we select more constraints in the regions where the deformation is high and must be minimized, but we still consider the regions where the deformation is small or none, by selecting a small number of constraints to represent them.

The affine transformation $A = [R|t]$, where R is a 3×3 rotation matrix and t is a 3D translation vector, is estimated for each node by a non-linear Gauss-Newton solver using the constraints selected previously. To store the affine transformations that will be estimated, we create two arrays: one array to store six parameters (i.e., 3 for quaternion and 3 for translation) for each node, and another array that is a hash relating a node in G to its parameters in the first array. We compute the array and the hash elements using atomic operations on the GPU.

The affine transformations computed in the previous step are applied on P_s and the algorithm is repeated, from the selection of nodes, until the maximum number of iterations is reached or the error becomes small.

To add support for non-rigid tracking, one solution is to apply it whenever the rigid tracking fails, enhancing the robustness of the MAR environment. However, to apply non-rigid tracking for a sequence of frames has a computational cost which does not make it suitable for real-time applications. Therefore, if rigid tracking keeps failing consecutively, non-rigid tracking will be used more frequently, decreasing application's performance.

To solve this problem, we take advantage from the volumetric representation of the KinectFusion algorithm to update the 3D reference model in real-time based on the current deformation measured, changing slightly the overview shown in Figure 5 to the one present in Figure 7. When the rigid tracking fails (i.e., error measured is above a certain threshold), non-rigid registration is applied and the 3D reference model deformed surface is sent to KinectFusion's grid. 3D reference model is updated in the grid representation by the TSDF computation and then the grid is ray casted to generate a new source surface for the next iteration. High weights during TSDF computation are used for fast adaptation of the previously stored 3D reference model into a new deformed one. As consequence, by deforming the 3D reference model, non-rigid tracking converges faster and with higher accuracy in the next iterations than the rigid-only solution (i.e., in which only rigid tracking is applied and KinectFusion's volume is not updated).

It is worthy to mention that non-rigid tracking is only performed for the target model (i.e., patient) being tracked in the multi-view environment (Section 3.). For the observer (i.e., physician), we do not employ non-rigid tracking by assuming that he will perform only rigid movements.

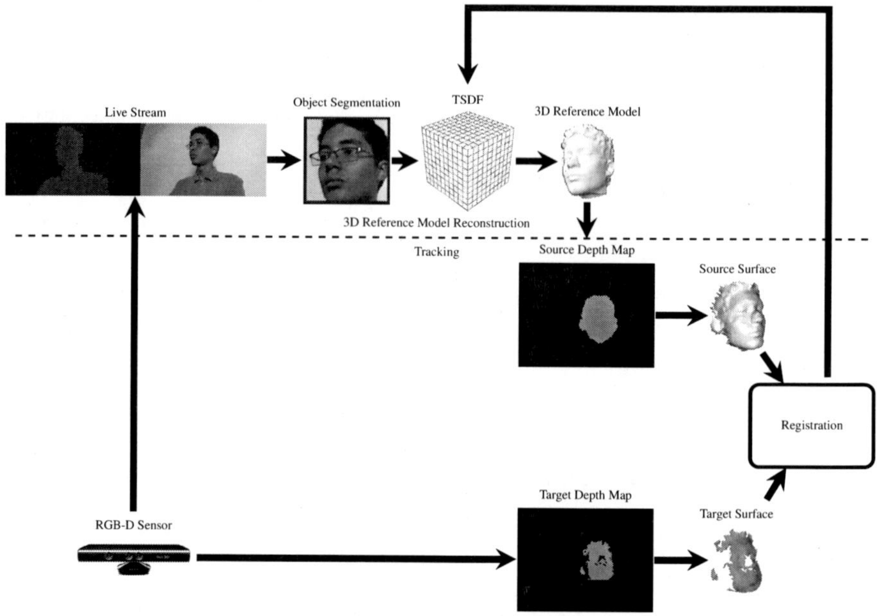

Figure 7. Revised overview of the proposed approach from 3D reference model reconstruction to non-rigid tracking solution.

4.4. On-Patient Volumetric Medical Data Visualization

Building upon the markerless tracking algorithm presented in the subsection 4.1., we use the environment for visualization of volumetric medical data on the patient, proposed in [44–47], and illustrated in Figure 8. Based on the previous 3D reference model reconstructed from the patient's ROI, the medical volume is rendered and positioned in the augmented scene. Instead of superimposing it over the patient's color image captured by the color sensor, our approach supports the use of four F+C visualization techniques to improve visual understanding of the scene.

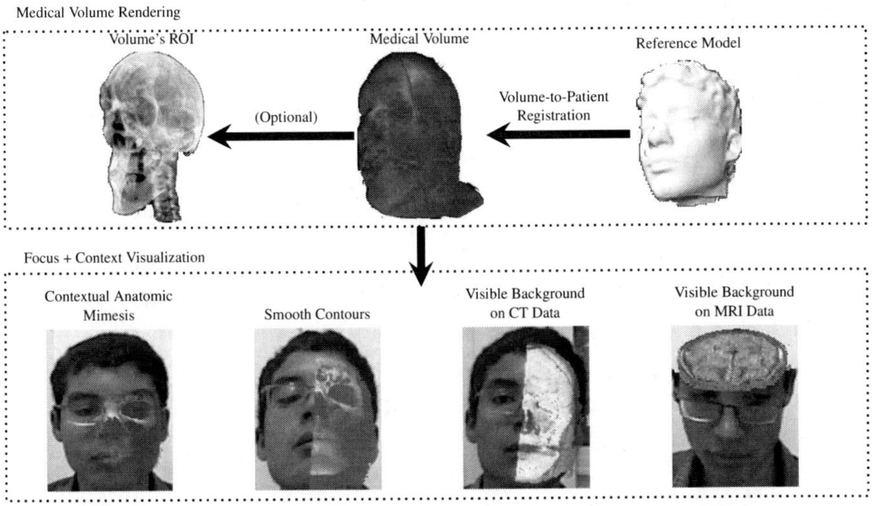

Figure 8. Overview of the on-patient medical data visualization solution proposed in this chapter.

4.4.1. Volume Rendering

Volume rendering is a field concerned with techniques for generating images from volume data [59]. As the scalar values stored in the volume data represent some physical property, transfer functions are commonly applied over these scalar values to improve user's visual perception by mapping the values to colors in RGB space. In this sense, we use pre-integrated transfer functions to capture the high frequencies introduced in the transfer functions with low sampling rates [60].

The technique most used for volume rendering is the ray casting algorithm [61–63]. One of the main advantages of this method is that it is flexible in the sense that many other techniques can be integrated to improve performance or image quality of the rendering.

To render the medical volume, we employ the most common techniques to optimize performance of the volume rendering: empty space skipping, adaptive sampling and early ray termination. For empty space skipping, the volume is subdivided into an octree. In order to detect empty spaces, each block stores the minimum and maximum scalar values. The visibility of each block can be determined after evaluation of the transfer function [64]. If the block is considered invisible, the step size of the ray can be increased, skipping the region where it is already known that there is not relevant data to be processed. Otherwise, by using adaptive sampling, the step size of the ray can be adaptively decreased to compute accurately the composition scheme. Early ray termination stops ray traversal if the opacity accumulated is too high, situation in which the contribution of new samples is irrelevant for the final rendering.

To improve image quality, we employ several techniques. To reduce sampling artifacts, stochastic jittering (i.e., random ray-start off-setting) is applied to the ray start position. To reduce the filtering artifacts, fast GPU-Based tri-cubic filtering [65,66] and GPU pre-filter are used for accurate tri-cubic filtering [67], replacing native tri-linear filtering.

To extract and emphasize important parts of a volume, our approach supports: volume clipping, which cuts away unimportant regions of the volume according to one of six planes parallel to the faces of the volume bounding box [59] and context-preserving volume rendering, which uses a function of: shading intensity, gradient magnitude, distance to the eye point and previously accumulated opacity to not only enhance features of the volume, but also to separate some structures in the visualization, such as bones, soft tissue and organs (Figure 8) [48,49]

After volume rendering, the next step is the placement of the medical data into the scene (Figure 8). However, as will be discussed in the Section 5., in this work patient's ROI is augmented with a generic volumetric data instead of his own. Therefore, we do not use an automatic registration method. Instead, we have used a new method for coarse registration between medical volume and patient's 3D reference model [47]. Then, the result can be fine adjusted by the user. Scale and translation are computed based on patient's 3D reference model. Rotation is computed by using a pose estimator algorithm.

4.4.2. Focus + Context Visualization

An application for on-patient medical data visualization requires a special attention to the mixing between real (i.e., patient's image captured by the sensor) and virtual (i.e., patient's anatomy stored in the computer) entities of the AR environment. Instead of superimposing the virtual content onto patient's real image, a better solution is to show a part of the virtual anatomy as a focus region in the context of the patient's body. In this sense, our MAR environment support four state-of-the-art F+C visualization techniques (Figure 8).

The first technique proposed for F+C visualization in the field of on-patient medical data visualization was the Contextual Anatomic Mimesis (CAM) [12]. To improve depth perception in a medical AR application, focus point and radius are defined, acting like a mask in the AR scene, in which the medical data can be visualized only inside it. Based on user-controlled parameters such as curvature and distance fall-off, this method allows high-quality on-patient medical data visualization, as already proven in previous work [35, 36]. This method was integrated in our environment, as can be seen in Figure 8.

One of the issues related to the integration of the volume clipping into the AR environment is the presence of the visible edge located in the intersection between the volume and the clipping plane. As discussed in [12], it is desirable a smooth transition between the volume in the focus region and the rest of the AR scene. In order to achieve this goal, the smooth contours technique is used to add a smooth transition between the image resulting from volume clipping and the context region [45]. The gray-scaled image of the medical volume is binarized and contours are extracted by using the Sobel edge-detector filter. Gaussian filter is used to blur the contours, and the resulting blurred contours image is a mask that gives a weight to the blending between volume contours and the scene. The influence of the smooth contours to the final image can be seen in Figure 8. It is visible that such algorithm adds a smooth transition between the volume and the real scene.

In volume rendering, CT data can be used to enable the visualization of internal structures such as bones. In the case of a head, this structure can be the patient's skull. By designing an appropriate transfer function, the skull can be visualized apart from the soft tissue of the volume. In this situation, it is desirable to see the real background scene when looking at the region between the skull and the soft tissue itself, because both are context regions of the volume and the virtual background can be seen, depending on the transfer function chosen. To achieve such result, the method for visible background on CT data uses a binary image which contains only the soft tissue region to mix it with the background scene already captured [45]. Soft tissue region is separated from the bone region according to a user-defined gray intensity. By using this algorithm, we obtain results similar to the one present in Figure 8.

In an AR environment, the best way to visualize clipped MRI data, which contains data of patient's organs, is by clipping not only the volume, but also the corresponding region on patient's image (Figure 8). In this situation, it is more appropriate to see the background scene in the region of the medical data clipped. The technique for visible background on MRI data works similar to the technique for CT data, however it uses a binary image of the clipped patient's ROI to indicate whether the background image must be rendered instead of the color image captured by the sensor [45]. To perform the clipping over the patient's ROI, one can take advantage from the KinectFusion volumetric representation (i.e., where the 3D reference model is stored as a implicit surface) to clip the 3D reference model (and, consequently, patient's ROI) in a fast and efficient way.

5. Results

We have tested the proposed environment using an Intel® Core™ i7-3770K CPU@3.50Ghz, 8GB RAM, NVIDIA GeForce GTX 660. To implement the approach proposed in this chapter, we have used the open-source C++ implementation of the KinectFusion [21] released by the Point Cloud Library (PCL) project [70]. Also, OpenNI was applied to capture the depth and color stream provided by the Kinect sensor [71]. Object detection and segmentation were performed by calling the OpenCV library procedures [72]. We have implemented 3D reference model reconstruction and non-rigid registration in GPU by using the NVIDIA CUDA architecture [73].

User's head was reconstructed with KinectFusion using a grid with volume size of $70cm \times 70cm \times 140cm$ and resolution of 512^3. The medical dataset used is a CT volumetric data of a head from the Visible Human Project [74] of resolution $128 \times 256 \times 256$ and a MRI data of a head available in Volume Library [75] of resolution 256^3. Both datasets have typical resolutions of a head medical volume.

The 3D reference model reconstruction and rigid tracking runs in real-time, as well as the on-patient medical data visualization solution. Non-rigid tracking takes $\approx$ 60ms. However, as we make use of an adaptive approach to apply the non-rigid registration only when required, application has average frame rate decreases to 20 FPS, which still enables user's interactivity with the application.

Regarding the two approaches for multi-view environment, both methods are feasible but have limitations. On the approach that employs glasses and one Kinect, the reconstructed model remains aligned to what is shown on the glasses' video, according to the transformation based on the initial calibration and on the glasses' tracking information and optical flow. As expected, the result is not perfect due to the interferences suffered by the glasses and the normalization of its angle values (in order to reduce instabilities and noise). However, this method has shown to be reasonably fast (imperceptible delay) and works well if the movements are not so fast. On case of fast large range movements, the optical flow is not able to track enough feature points anymore and so the tracking is lost and needs to be restarted. For the second method, based on two Kinects, the glasses are still worn by the observer, since the lenses are used as output device and glasses' video is still used as background to be aligned with the reconstructed model. The initial alignment is the same as the first method, based on the calibration file, but for the next frames, the target model is transformed according to the transformation of the observer's model as calculated by the second Kinect. The alignment here is worse than the previous method, which can be explained by short range motion which is not perfectly perceived by Kinect. However, it works better for large range motion, although it can also lose track for fast movements. It also requires much more computational resources than the first method.

We evaluate the visual quality of the proposed environment in a scenario where patient's head is augmented with the volumetric dataset mentioned above. The use of a generic volume does not affect the visual quality of our environment since the volume is scaled and semi-automatically positioned by the user.

As can be seen in Figure 9, our approach supports occlusion at shader level. However, if the occluder overlaps more than 70% of the occludee, tracking may fail.

Influence of context-preserving volume rendering in our application can be seen in Figure 10. According to the technique proposed by Brucker et al. [48, 49], we can control the rendering of the medical data, emphasizing the visualization of internal (e.g., bone) or external structures (e.g., soft tissue). Support for this kind of rendering is specially important in our application, be-

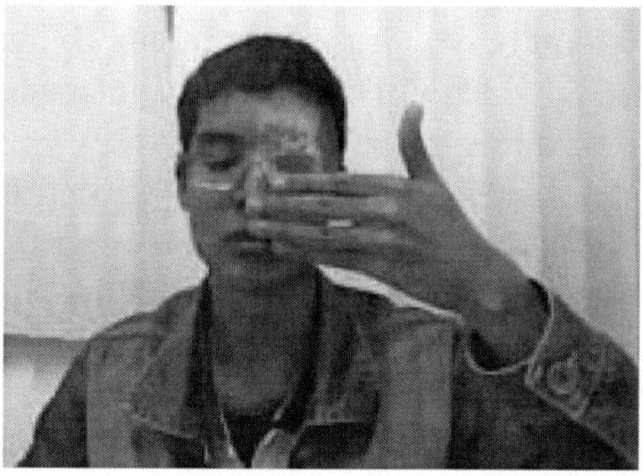

Figure 9. Occlusion support.

cause it enables the physician to control the visualization of the medical data.

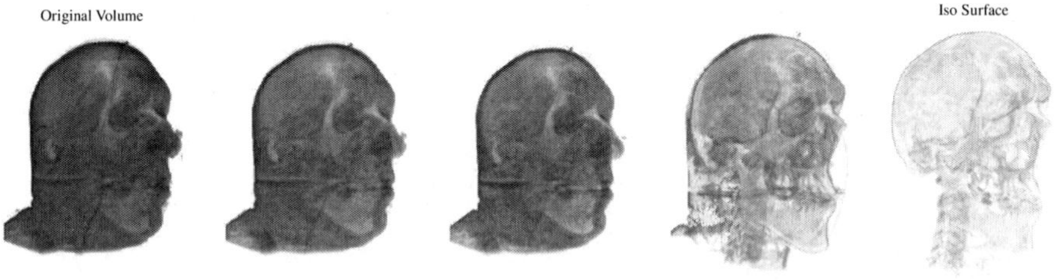

Figure 10. From volume to iso surface visualization by controlling context-preserving volume rendering parameters.

From Figure 11, we can see the CAM technique in our MAR environment. By defining a focus point and radius, the user can control which parts of the volume to visualize in the AR scene. Moreover, it is visible that the transition between real and virtual images is smooth.

F+C visualization based on smooth contours is illustrated in Figure 12. The algorithm effectively adds a smooth transition between the volume and the real scene at the region of the volume contours.

The Figure 13 shows the F+C visualization based on visible background on

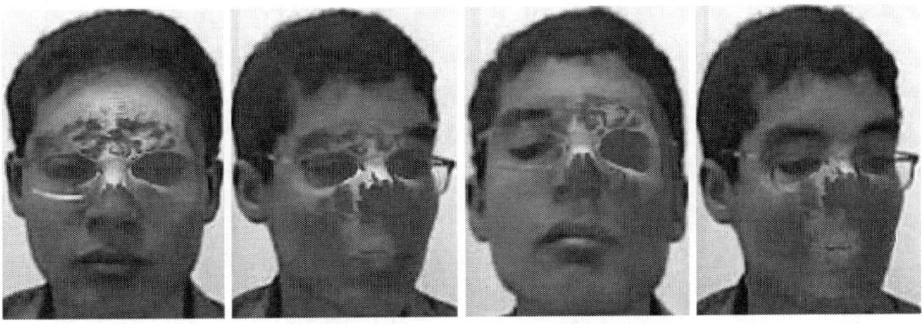

Figure 11. Contextual Anatomic Mimesis applied on our environment.

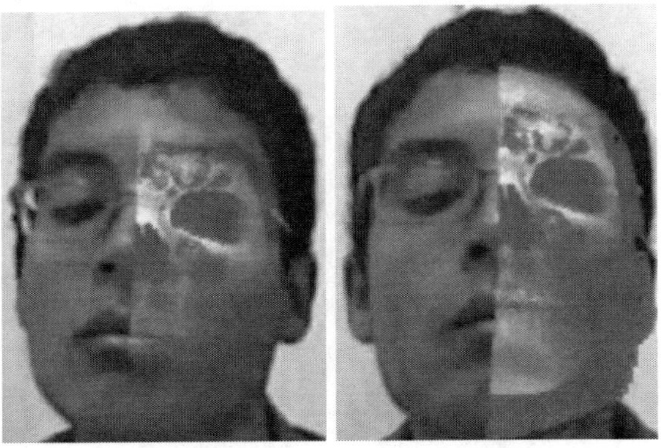

Figure 12. Focus + context visualization based on smooth contours.

CT data. We can notice that the technique allows the soft tissue to be rendered linearly interpolated with the background scene.

In Figure 14, we combine the F+C visualization based on visible background with MRI data. In the upper clipping, there is a good composition with the medical data in the scene. However, in the lateral clipping, it is visible the 3D reference model clipping and the background rendering because of the shadow cutting present on the final scene.

Related to the non-rigid tracking support, we have evaluated five situations where the user deformed his face in front of the sensor after 3D rigid recon-

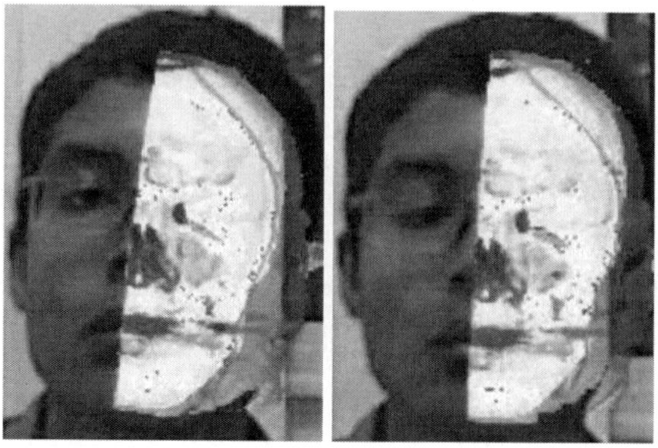

Figure 13. Visible background for Computed Tomography data.

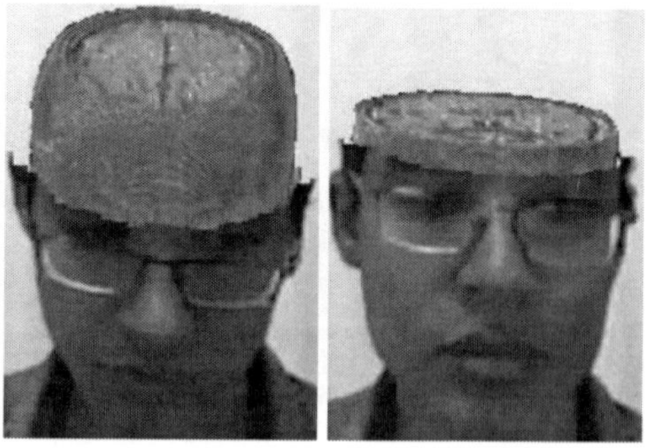

Figure 14. Examples of interactions with the F+C visualization based on visible background on MRI Data.

struction. To evaluate the proposed environment with respect to challenging deformation scenarios, we have tested the algorithm with different objects and in different conditions for deformation. In this case, we have asked one user to inflate his cheeks, smile and simulate a "kiss" expression, as shown in Figure 15.

Next, with a different user, we consider different deformations: open mouth and angry facial expressions, as can be seen in Figure 16. Compared to the pre-

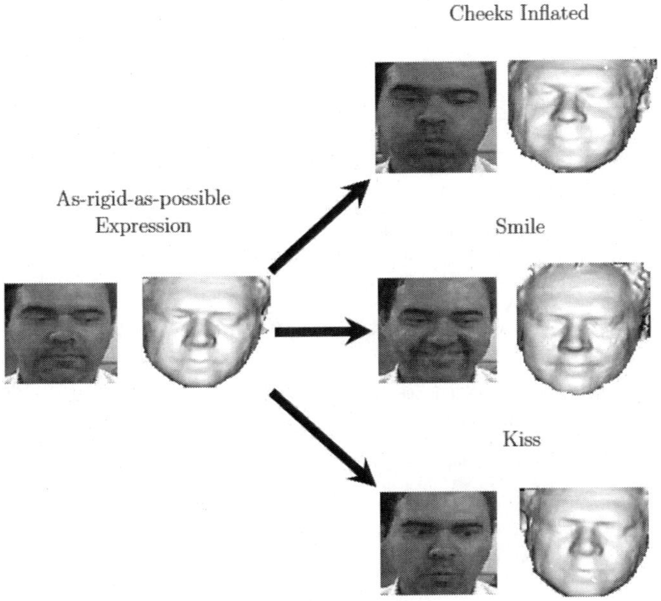

Figure 15. Neutral and deformed reference models for a different user.

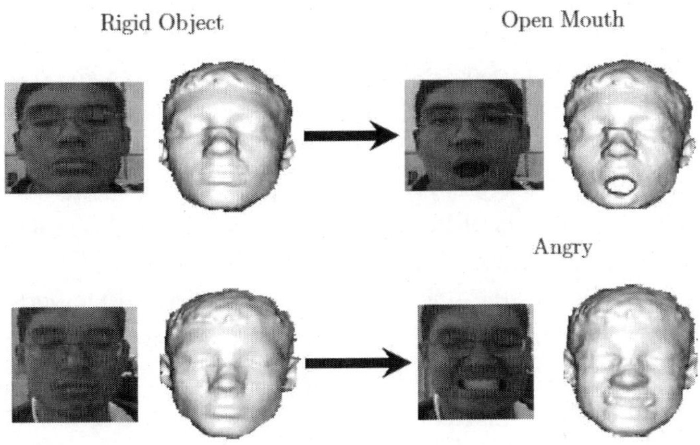

Figure 16. Neutral and deformed reference models based on challenging deformation scenarios.

vious scenarios, these deformations present additional challenges for the non-rigid registration algorithm:

- Open mouth expression poses a challenging scenario for matching of points, because the corresponding points become too distant during the motion of deformation. Also, there is a big hole on the deformed model which makes the process of matching even more difficult;
- Angry expression has higher tracking error than open mouth expression, however it introduces less holes in the deformed model.

Despite of the mentioned challenges, the Figures 15 and 16 show that non-rigid tracking can be successfully performed by deforming the 3D reference model to the current pose done by the user.

6. Conclusion

In this chapter we have present an integrated multi-view markerless augmented reality environment for on-patient medical data visualization based on focus + context visualization, rigid and non-rigid tracking. From an evaluation of the proposed solution, we conclude that it runs in real-time on typical medical datasets, providing high visual quality for the final augmented scene through the use of focus + context visualization. When used, non-rigid tracking enhanced the robustness of the algorithm while still allowing real-time performance.

Although the solution presented in this chapter was evaluated only for a scenario where the region of interest is a head, we believe that with minor adaptations the method could track other regions of the body with enough accuracy due to the capabilities of the ICP and KinectFusion based methods [20, 21]. However, experiments must still be conducted to evaluate if the accuracy achieved is enough for medical AR applications to aid surgery, for instance.

In terms of limitation, our approach does not support relocalization and tracking fails if patient's ROI is not visible in the scene. Therefore, it is possible to improve tracking robustness by solving these issues. F+C visualization based on visible background techniques do not support the visualization of real dynamic background scenes. We can take advantage of the multi-view environment in order to address such issue by using an additional webcam to capture real background scene. Another possibility for future works is to extend the current application to support photorealism, taking into account global illumination effects into the volume rendering. Performance for non-rigid tracking can be improved by using optimized solutions for the non-linear optimization algorithm, as proposed in [32], or by using an hybrid approach for distributing processing in both GPU and multi-threaded CPU, as done in [31].

References

[1] Akenine-Moller, T.; Moller, T.; Haines, E. Real-Time Rendering; A. K. Peters: Natick, MA, 2002; Vol. 2.

[2] Kato, H.; Billinghurst, M. Marker Tracking and HMD Calibration for a Video-based Augmented Reality Conferencing System. IWAR, 1999, 85-94.

[3] Fiala, M. ARTag, A Fiducial Marker System Using Digital Techniques. CVPR, 2005, 590-596.

[4] Koyama, T. Introduction to FLARToolKit. Adobe System Incorporated. 2009.

[5] Souza, R. C.; Moreira, H. D. F.; Kirner, C. FLARAS 1.0–Flash Augmented Reality Authoring System. 2012.

[6] Pilet, J.; Lepetit, V.; Fua, P. Fast Non-Rigid Surface Detection, Registration and Realistic Augmentation. Int. J. Comput. Vision. 2008, vol. 76, 109-122.

[7] Gay-Bellile, V.; Bartoli, A.; Sayd, P. Direct Estimation of NonRigid Registration with Image-Based Self-Occlusion Reasoning. IEEE Trans. Pattern Anal. Mach. Intell. 2010, vol. 32, 87-104.

[8] Uchiyama, H.; Marchand, E. Deformable Random Dot Markers. ISMAR, 2011, 237-238.

[9] Azuma, R. T. A Survey of Augmented Reality. Presence-Teleop. Virt. 1997, vol. 6, 355-385.

[10] Muller, M.; Rassweiler, M-C.; Klein, J.; Seitel, A.; Gondan, M.; Baumhauer, M.; Teber, D.; Rassweiler, J.J.; Meinzer, H.-P.; Maier-Hein, L. Mobile Augmented Reality for Computer-Assisted Percutaneous Nephrolithotomy. Int. J. Comput. Assist. Radiol. Surg.. 2013, vol. 8, 663-675.

[11] Card, S. K.; Mackinlay, J. D.; Shneiderman, B. Readings in Information Visualization: Using Vision to Think; Morgan Kaufmann Publishers Inc: San Francisco, CA, 1999.

[12] Bichlmeier, C.; Wimmer, F.; Heining, S. M.; Navab, N. Contextual Anatomic Mimesis Hybrid In-Situ Visualization Method for Improving Multi-Sensory Depth Perception in Medical Augmented Reality. ISMAR, 2007, 1-10.

[13] Azuma, R. T. Predictive Tracking for Augmented Reality. University of North Carolina at Chapel Hill: Chapel Hill, NC, 1995.

[14] Azuma, R.; Baillot, Y.; Behringer, R.; Feiner, S.; Julier, S.; MacIntyre, B. Recent Advances in Augmented Reality. IEEE Comput. Graph. Appl. 2001, vol. 21, 34-47

[15] Wagner, D.; Schmalstieg, D. ARToolKitPlus for Pose Tracking on Mobile Devices. CVWW, 2007.

[16] Nowrouzezahrai, D.; Geiger, S.; Mitchell, K.; Sumner, R.; Jarosz, W.; Gross, M. Light Factorization for Mixed-Frequency Shadows in Augmented Reality. ISMAR, 2011, 173-179.

[17] Oskam, T.; Hornung, A.; Sumner, R.W.; Gross, M. Fast and Stable Color Balancing for Images and Augmented Reality. 3DIMPVT, 2012, 49-56.

[18] Myojin, S.; Sato, A.; Shimada, N. Augmented Reality Card Game Based on User-Specific Information Control. MM, 2012, 1193-1196.

[19] Teichrieb, V.; Paulo, J.; Silva, M. L.; Apolinario, E. L.; Souto, T.; Cordeiro, M.; Farias, M.; Bueno, A. S.; Kelner, J.; Santos, I. H. F. A Survey of Online Monocular Markerless Augmented Reality. Int. J. Model. Sim. Petrol. Ind., 2007, vol. 1, 1-7.

[20] Rusinkiewicz, S.; Levoy, M. Efficient Variants of the ICP Algorithm. 3DIM, 2001, 145-152.

[21] Izadi, S.; Kim, D.; Hilliges, O.; Molyneaux, D.; Newcombe, R.; Kohli, P.; Shotton, J.; Hodges, S.; Freeman, D.; Davidson, A.; Fitzgibbon, A. KinectFusion: Real-time 3D Reconstruction and Interaction Using a Moving Depth Camera. UIST, 2011, 559-568.

[22] Macedo, M. C. F.; Apolinario, A. L.; Souza, A. C. S. A Robust Real-Time Face Tracking Using Head Pose Estimation for a Markerless AR System. SVR, 2014, 224-227.

[23] Macedo, M. C. F.; Apolinario, A. L.; Souza, A. C. S. A Markerless Augmented Reality Approach Based on Real-Time 3D Reconstruction using Kinect. SIBGRAPI, 2013.

[24] Macedo, M. C. F.; Apolinario, A. L.; Souza, A. C. S. KinectFusion for Faces: Real-Time 3D Face Tracking and Modeling Using a Kinect Camera for a Markerless AR System. J. Interact. Syst. 2013, vol. 4, 2-7.

[25] Sumner, R. W.; Schmid, J.; Pauly, M. Embedded Deformation for Shape Manipulation. ACM Trans. Graph, 2007, vol. 26.

[26] Li, H.; Sumner, R. W.; Pauly, M. Global Correspondence Optimization for Non-Rigid Registration of Depth Scans. SGP, 2008.

[27] Li, H.; Adams, B.; Guibas, L. J., Pauly, M. Robust Single-View Geometry And Motion Reconstruction. ACM Trans. Graph, 2009, vol. 28.

[28] Li, H.; Luo, L.; Vlasic, D.; Peers, P.; Popovic, J.; Pauly, M.; Rusinkiewicz, S. Temporally Coherent Completion of Dynamic Shapes. ACM Trans. Graph, 2012, vol. 31.

[29] Dou, M.; Fuchs, H.; Frahm, J-M. Scanning and Tracking Dynamic Objects with Commodity Depth Cameras. ISMAR, 2013.

[30] Chen, J.; Izadi, S.; Fitzgibbon, A. KinETre: Animating the World with the Human Body. UIST, 2012, 435-444.

[31] Nutti, B.; Kronander, A.; Nilsing, M.; Maad, K.; Svensson, C.; Li, H. Depth Sensor-Based Realtime Tumor Tracking for Accurate Radiation Therapy. Eurographics, 2014.

[32] Zollhofer, M.; Niessner, M.; Izadi, S.; Rehmann, C.; Zach, C.; Fisher, M.; Wu, C.; Fitzgibbon, A.; Loop, C.; Theobalt, C.; Stamminger, M. Real-time Non-rigid Reconstruction using an RGB-D Camera. ACM Trans. Graph., 2014.

[33] Souza, A. C. S.; Macedo, M. C. F.; Apolinario, A. L. Multi-Frame Adaptive Non-Rigid Registration for Markerless Augmented Reality. VRCAI, 2014, 7-16.

[34] Souza, A. C. S.; Macedo, M. C. F.; Apolinario, A. L. A GPU-Based Adaptive Algorithm for Non-Rigid Surface Registration. VR, 2015.

[35] Kutter, O.; Aichert, A.; Bichlmeier, C.; Traub, J.; Heining, S. M.; Ockert, B.; Euler, E.; Navab, N. Real-Time Volume Rendering for High Quality Visualization in Augmented Reality. AMI-ARCS, 2008.

[36] Wieczorek, M.; Aichert, A.; Kutter, O.; Bichlmeier, C.; Landes, J.; Heining, S. M.; Euler, E.; Navab, N. GPU-accelerated Rendering for Medical Augmented Reality in Minimally-Invasive Procedures. BVM, 2010.

[37] Lee, J-D.; Huang, C-H.; Huang, T-C.; Hsieh, H-Y.; Lee, S-T. Medical Augment Reality Using a Markerless Registration Framework. Expert Syst. Appl. 2012, vol. 39, 5286-5294.

[38] Blum, T.; Kleeberger, V.; Bichlmeier, C.; Navab, N. Mirracle: An Augmented Reality Magic Mirror System for Anatomy Education. VR, 2012, 169-170.

[39] Meng, M.; Fallavollita, P.; Blum, T.; Eck, U.; Sandor, C.; Weidert, S.; Waschke, J.; Navab, N. Kinect for Interactive AR anatomy learning. ISMAR, 2013, 277-278.

[40] Stefan, P.; Wucherer, P.; Oyamada, Y.; Ma, M.; Schoch, A.; Kanegae, M.; Shimizu, N.; Kodera, T.; Cahier, S.; Weigl, M.; Sugimoto, M.; Fallavollita, P.; Saito, H.; Navab, N. An AR Edutainment System Supporting Bone Anatomy Learning. VR, 2014, 113-114.

[41] Mercier-Ganady, J.; Lotte, F.; Loup-Escande, E.; Marchal, M.; Lecuyer, A. The Mind-Mirror: See Your Brain in Action in Your Head Using EEG and Augmented Reality. VR, 2014, 33-38.

[42] Kilgus, T.; Heim, E.; Haase, S.; PrÃ¼fer, S.; MÃ¼ller, M.; Seitel, A.; Fangerau, M.; Wiebe, T.; Iszatt, J.; Schlemmer, H-P.; Hornegger, J.; Yen, K.; Maier-Hein, L. Mobile Markerless Augmented Reality and its Application in Forensic Medicine. Int. J. Comput. Assist. Radiol. Surg., 2014, 1-14.

[43] Maier-Hein, L.; Franz, A. M.; Fangerau, M.; Schmidt, M.; Seitel, A.; Mersmann, S.; Kilgus, T.; Groch, A.; Yung, K.; dos Santos, T. R.; Meinzer, H-P. Towards Mobile Augmented Reality for On-Patient Visualization of Medical Images. BVM, 2011, 389-393.

[44] Macedo, M. C. F.; Apolinario, A. L.; Souza, A. C. S.; Giraldi, G. A. A Semi-automatic Markerless Augmented Reality Approach for On-Patient Volumetric Medical Data Visualization. SVR, 2014, 63-70.

[45] Macedo, M. C. F.; Apolinario, A. L. Improving On-Patient Medical Data Visualization in a Markerless Augmented Reality Environment by Volume Clipping. SIBGRAPI, 2014, 149-156.

[46] Macedo, M. C. F.; Almeida, C.; Souza, A. C. S. ; Silva, J.; Apolinario, A. L.; Giraldi, G. A. A Markerless Augmented Reality Environment for Medical Data Visualization. WIM, 2014, 1682-1691.

[47] Macedo, M. C. F.; Apolinario, A. L.; Souza, A. C.; Giraldi, G. A. High-Quality On-Patient Medical Data Visualization in a Markerless Augmented Reality Environment. J. Interact. Syst. 2014, vol. 5, 41-52.

[48] Bruckner, S.; Grimm, S.; Kanitsar, A.; Gröller, M. E. Illustrative Context-preserving Volume Rendering. EUROVIS. 2005. 69-76.

[49] Bruckner, S.; Grimm, S.; Kanitsar, A.; Gröller, M. E. Illustrative Context-Preserving Exploration of Volume Data. TVCG. 2006. 1559-1569.

[50] Almeida, C. S. B. A Multi-View Environment for Markerless Augmented Reality. Federal University of Bahia. 2014.

[51] Almeida, C. S. B.; Apolinario, A. L.. A proposal of a multi-view environment for markerless augmented reality. SIBGRAPI, 2013.

[52] Cruz, L.; Lucio, D.; Velho, L. Kinect and RGBD Images: Challenges and Applications. SIBGRAPI. 2014. 36-49.

[53] Viola, P.; Jones, M. J. Robust Real-Time Face Detection. Int. J. Comput. Vision., 2004, vol. 57, 137-154.

[54] Tomasi, C.; Manduchi, R. Bilateral Filtering for Gray and Color Images. ICCV, 1998, 839-846.

[55] Osher, S. J.; Fedkim, R. P. Level Set Methods and Dynamic Implicit Surfaces. Springer, 2002.

[56] Fanelli, G.; Weise, T.; Gall, J.; van Gool, L. Real Time Head Pose Estimation from Consumer Depth Cameras. DAGM, 2011.

[57] Lucas, B. D.; Kanade, T. An Iterative Image Registration Technique with an Application to Stereo Vision. IJCAI, 1981, 674-679.

[58] Shi, J.; Tomasi, C. Good Features to Track. CVPR, 1994, 593-600.

[59] Hadwiger, M.; Kniss, J. M.; Rezk-Salama, C.; Weiskopf, D.; Engel, K. Real-Time Volume Graphics. A. K. Peters, Ltd. 2006.

[60] Engel, K.; Kraus, M.; Ertl, T. High-Quality Pre-Integrated Volume Rendering using Hardware-Accelerated Pixel Shading. HWWS, 2001, 9-16.

[61] Levoy, M. Display of Surfaces from Volume Data. IEEE Comput. Graph. Appl. 1988, vol. 8, 29-37.

[62] Kruger, J.; Westermann, R. Acceleration Techniques for GPU-based Volume Rendering. VIS, 2003.

[63] Roettger, S.; Guthe, S.; Weiskopf, D.; Ertl, T.; Strasser, W. Smart Hardware-Accelerated Volume Rendering. VISSYM, 2003, 231-238.

[64] Li, W.; Mueller, K.; Kaufman, A. Empty Space Skipping and Occlusion Clipping for Texture-based Volume Rendering. VIS, 2003, 317-324.

[65] Sigg, C.; Hadwiger, M. Fast Third-Order Texture Filtering. GPU Gems 2, 2005, 313-329.

[66] Ruijters, D.; ter Haar Romeny, B. M.; Suetens, P. Efficient GPU-Based Texture Interpolation using Uniform B-Splines. J. Graphics Tools. 2008, vol. 13, 61-69.

[67] Ruijters, D.; Thevenaz, P. GPU Prefilter for Accurate Cubic B-spline Interpolation. Comput. J. 2012, vol. 55, 15-20.

[68] Glocker, B.; Izadi, S.; Shotton, J.; Criminisi, A. Real-Time RGB-D Camera Relocalization. ISMAR, 2013, 173-179.

[69] Glocker, B.; Shotton, J.; Criminisi, A.; Izadi, S. Real-Time RGB-D Camera Relocalization via Randomized Ferns for Keyframe Encoding. TVCG, 2014.

[70] Rusu, R. B.; Cousins, S. 3D is here: Point Cloud Library (PCL). ICRA, 2011, 1-4.

[71] Occipital (2015). OpenNI. http://structure.io/openni

[72] Bradski, G. R.; Kaehler, A. Learning Opencv. O'Reilly Media, Inc. 2008.

[73] Kirk, D. B.; Hwu, W. W. Programming Massively Parallel Processors: A Hands-on Approach. Morgan Kaufmann Publishers Inc.: San Francisco, CA. 2010.

[74] National Library of Medicine (2014). Visible Human Data. http://www.nlm.nih.gov/research/visible/.

[75] Volume Library (2014). Volume Library. http://www9.informatik.uni-erlangen.de/External/vollib/.

In: Augmented Reality
Editor: Raymond Hughes
ISBN: 978-1-63482-902-1

Chapter 4

CONSUMERS AUGMENTED EXPERIENCE AND DIGITAL ENGAGEMENT TOOLS: SOME EVIDENCES

***Maria Teresa Cuomo*[1,•], *Gerardino Metallo*[1,*], *Valentina Scannapieco*[2,#] and *Debora Tortora*[3,¥]**
[1]Dept. of Business Studies and Research, University of Salerno, Italy
[2]Managerial and marketing consultant, Blogger, Italy
[3]Dept. of Economics and Statistics, University of Salerno, Italy

ABSTRACT

In the actual hypercompetitive and unsure economic contest firms must necessarily make attention to new opportunities given by the social exchanges, i.e., the growth of internet connection in store by smartphones, in order to increase the chances to succeed or simply to survive in the market.

Nowadays consumers strongly need to express themselves, to create relationship, and to have value exchanges. Therefore firms could gain success by setting up an emotive and passionate dialogue with them, by means of a new interactive marketing approach. New technologies and social media allow continuous contacts between firms and users and,

• E-mail: mcuomo@unisa.it.
* E-mail: gemetall@unisa.it.
# E-mail: va.scaneco@gmail.com.
¥ E-mail: dtortora@unisa.it.

consequently, they improve mutual knowledge. Even the customer experience changes and evolves thanks to the support of new technologies, into and off stores. While e-commerce apparently threatens traditional trade, stores realize that competitive prices, suitable goods selection and additional services are not enough to attract and hold consumers back. In this light, recent studies underline as users are more likely to buy when they have involving interaction with brands and engagement in stores. Thus, capitalising on user's digital knowledge, firms try to exploit this trend to their advantage. In this context, augmented reality, that is the application of virtual elements in a real dimension, conceived as strategic tool, supports the creation of brand engagement through immersive customer experiences and improve firms' turnover. In spite of this, the phenomenon is not immune to problems and limits which, after a thorough analysis of augmented reality both from a theoretical and empirical point of view, will be extensively encountered and discussed in the present chapter.

Keywords: augmented marketing, retailing, ecommerce, content brand perceptions

1. Interactive Contexts and Augmented Communication

At the present time, it is evident that brand knowledge, reliability, communication and widespread diffusion are no longer sufficient to guarantee a brand's success. Consumers require total involvement in the consumption experience, and the governance of brand interaction has to be redefined ad hoc in the specific socio-constructed spaces of the environment, technology, service and sociality mix. On the other hand, recent researches (Scatena, Mardegan, 2012) indicate a positive and significant correlation between levels of engagement promoted by a brand and annual turnover and profits achieved by the firm, especially during a recession. Consequently, marketers are continually in search for new opportunities of approaching and involving clients, particularly in brand terms. A critical success factor for achieving this mainly emotional feeling between brand and consumer can be envisaged in the so-called "P factor" (passion) seen as a new communicational client approach, producing its effects internally and externally to the brand, since the development of a passion-related brand is essentially explicated in the leap (conceptual and performance-wise) of customer satisfaction, generated from zero defect solutions to customer delight and classified in terms of zero defection. The dimensions which strongly influence the relevance of the brand-consumer relationship can be classified into: competence, as the result of experience in terms of the qualitative superiority or excellence of the brand, where the customer's income potential (share of wallet) is in direct reference to his/her link with the offer, as occurs typically for symbolic brands; protagonism, in terms of perceived success and expected capacity by means of which the brand communicates through a sort of institutional promise capable of prevaricating the fame of its relative products; affinity, summed up in terms of brand personality and consonance with the customer's lifestyle, which abandons a purely commercial dimension of the relation, and consequently governs relevant desires and emotional implications (Cuomo et al., 2009, p. 242).

In such manner, a pervasive status in which the brand sustains values that are shared with customers, in a passion-related perspective in consumer terms, guarantees the brand a consolidated and above all lasting place in terms of income. In this perspective, customization and exclusivity of the message and the timeliness, placing and contextualizing of the user experience are already becoming essential elements of the media platforms for repositioning products in the sense and value making process. In these terms, within the interactive and cooperative dynamics of the web, brand (and corporate generally) communication has benefited enormously from the contamination between traditional tools and information technology, welcoming customer involvement, interaction and active participation in the search for integration of on the spot content and shared collective, non-codified knowledge. A pertinent example is that of storytelling, as a narrative approach to (external) communication for the conveying of firm/brand value, promoting cooperation and widespread knowledge (Lundqvist et al., 2013, p. 285). The tool has found a narrative declination of greater emotional and value impact in digital storytelling by virtue of its bi-univocal dimension that transforms the story into conversation, or in other words, on the spot or spontaneous customer-brand communication. In its virtual dimension the narrative expedient unfolds along three poles: information, participation and, links to satisfy the desire of many actors (consumers, visitors, etc.) to have their say, amplifying and spreading their voice through the various tools and media.

Therefore, augmented reality (AR) – as an addition of information in real environments, since 3D virtual objects are integrated into a 3D real environment in real time, enhancing the user's perception of and interaction with the real world (Azuma, 1997) – offers corporate communication a kind of "fourth spatial dimension" that intersects the poles mentioned above, for a completely new dilated brand experience (see figure 1).

Thus, in order to survive in this "new age of marketing" businesses have to identify strategies of (digital) engagement, i.e., change their interaction tactics with consumers within a graded scale of persuasion, relations, experience and sharing. Recent empirical studies (Trubow, Mattew, 2013) underline a positive correlation between customer involvement, by means of augmented advertising campaigns, and purchasing (see table 1, elaboration by the Authors from www.arblog.inglobetechnologies.com) and between brand engagement and turnover and margin of the firms.

More in detail, comparing a traditional marketing campaign with another based on augmented reality, both of them promoting the same offer (children's construction toy) and brand, augmented advertising seems to be more effective than traditional one.

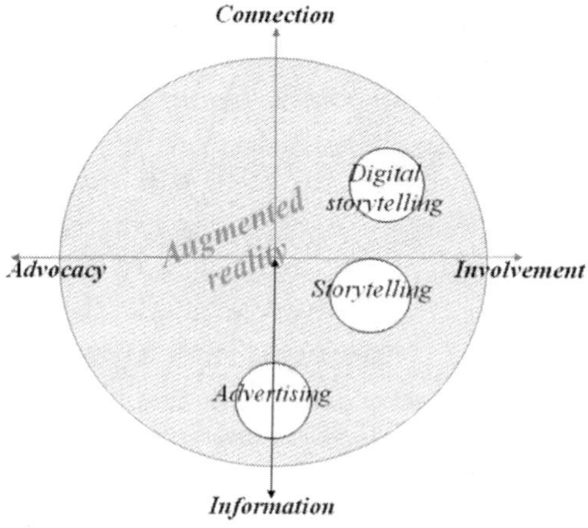

Figure 1. Tools for promoting consumer involvement.

Table 1. Comparative analysis of traditional to augmented marketing

Variables	Traditional mktg	Augmented mktg	% Variation
Time	12 seconds	83 seconds	+ 591%
Intention to buy	45%	74%	+ 64%
Price consideration	5.99 pounds	7.99 pounds	+ 33.38%
Offer value	-	-	+ 33%

Most effectiveness stems from the fact that augmented reality stimulates emotional interactions between product and user, making possible the virtual contact and the test of the offer before purchasing, or expanding it with new elements, creating by this way an emotional link that increases customers' intention to buy. Therefore, by means of augmented reality marketers can define new opportunities to customer approach and involvement, in terms of personalization, timeliness, localization and contextualization of the brand user experience, also redefining the process of sense and value making.

2. The Augmented Consumption

Technological innovation pushes towards a contextual sophistication and simplification in terms of the information and communication devices. Systems are at the same time more elaborate but also accessible – not only to the digital natives – leading people to a deep metamorphosis, in behavioral and relational terms. The changes provoked by digital revolution and the increasing degree of contamination in the communication system affect their own perception as users. By one hand, user considers himself relieved from materiality thanks to the effect of virtualization of contacts, friendship and so on. On the other hand he appears irreversibly blocked in the maze of technological innovation and enslaved to its trends in terms of consumption, communication and relationships, too.

An event among others testifies this evolution, that is the increase of e-commerce, growing up 17% during 2014 in Italy with a value of 13.3 billion euros (e-Commerce B2C Netcomm Observatory, Politecnico of Milan), especially by means of mobile devices (http://visual.ly/predictions-mobile-ecommerce-2014) (see figure 2).

In actual fact, according to a new forecast from the International Data Corporation, the combined total market of smartphones, tablets plus 2-in-1s, and PCs is set to grow from 1.8 billion units in 2014 to 2.5 billion units in 2019. During that time, smartphones will grow to represent the overwhelming majority of total smart connected device (SCD) shipments (International Data Corporation, 2015). Hence, considering their potential use in the retail sector, smartphones already constitute devices capable of governing enabling mechanisms, destined to create/stimulate stories about the products, excite interest and generate shelf emotions/experiences, creating new modes of interaction between individuals and the surrounding reality in terms of consumer experience.

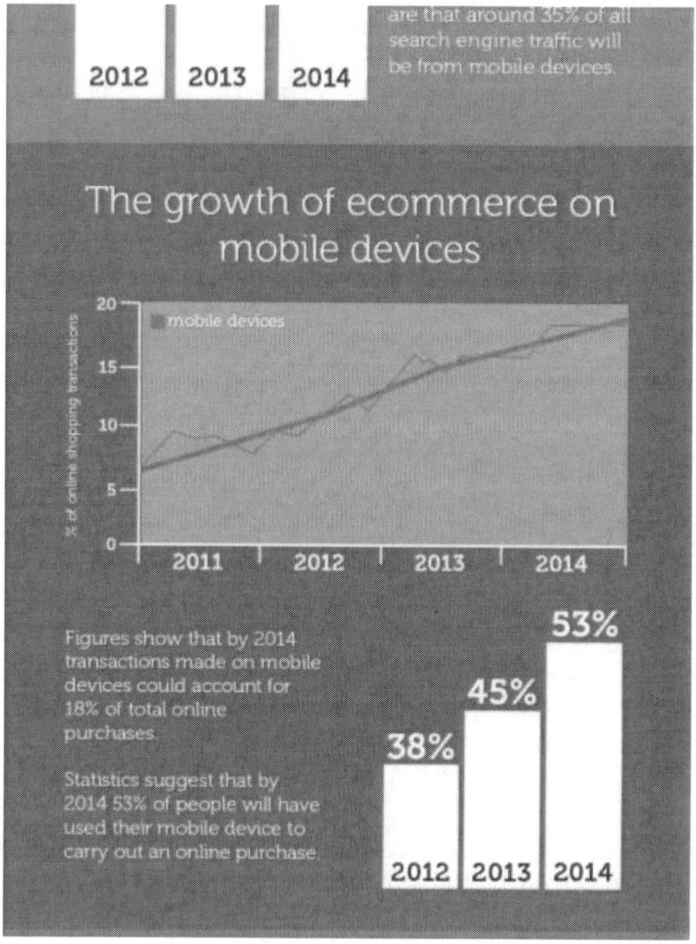

Figure 2. *Predictions for Mobile E-commerce 2014.*

Consequently, mobile marketing as "the use of wireless media as an integrated content delivery and direct-response vehicle within a cross-media marketing communications program" (Venkatesh, 2015, p. 1177) supports and emphasizes two/(or many)-way communications, using some characteristics to engage consumers, as sociality, responsiveness, locally reference, video entertainment (Brognara, 2014); in the sum, it has the ability to put brands in consumer hands, and eventually in its shopping cart in a real time. Effectively, the co-existing of functional and emotional factors is acknowledged in the studies on the mobile internet, mobile data service, mobile multimedia service and location-based mobile service (Varnali, Toker, 2010).

Thanks to these technological supports, the offer/brand enriches itself of extra-contents (both informational and sensorial), amplifies its significance toward consumers and inflects its commercial and emotional charm through new dimensions. In the post social era, market experiences the transition from the Digital Convergence, based on the combination of voice, text, imagines, media streaming and personalized services, to the Convergence Augmentation, with the meeting of digital environment and real word in a comprising context (Hoffman, Novak, 2012).

Although its "technological complexity", collecting and analyzing information before purchase becomes more "timely and eased", with the result of contracting the customer decision-making process and nearly deleting the post-purchase cognitive dissonance. In effect in 2014, 60 million users at least exploited augmented reality applications by tablet, glasses and smartphones above all (Juniper Research Report, 2014 - see table 2).

Table 2. Diffusion and use of smartphones in Italy

	Smartphone penetration compared with population	Smartphone users searching information by their device
	41%	92%
2014, Italy		
	Smartphone users coming in touch with products by their smartphones	Smartphone users purchasing by their smartphones
	84%	30%

In short, the increasing use of augmented reality applications encourages a greater number of firms to make available these tools to their customers.

First appearing in the literature in the 1940s but becoming widespread only in the late 1980s, augmented reality (used in 1992 by the researcher Thomas Preston Caudell, a Boeing engineer, to describe a system of new generation technology for assembling and installing electric cables in airplanes – Caudell e Mizell, 1992) indicated «a term for a camera enhanced view of a physical real-world environment, where virtual elements are merged with the real-life scenes creating a "mixed reality" of virtual elements and the real world» (Trubow, 2011a, p. 4). In other words, a monitor and a video are sufficient to integrate real life into a virtual context. Sure enough, the augmented reality system – combining the real world with the virtual world and generating augmented scene, being interactive, allowing registration of virtual objects to corresponding real objects – can be installed and accessed in a desktop computer, smartphones or can be projected through any kind of supporting display systems (Raajan et al., 2013).

In any event, although seen as the extreme end of a continuum, compared to Virtual Reality (VR), in which information added or removed electronically is predominant and the consumer is led towards a "cancelling" perception of his emotional exploring of the context or situation, in Augmented Reality, purchaser perceptions are solicited by the addition of information and emotional levels (through multimedia content, i.e., video, audio and animations), enjoyed "unrestrictedly", and at the same time, transferable to other users – once modified by the former, who has meanwhile in his turn, added virtual content (see figure 3).

Such content in transit towards social media platforms, generates links with the brand – adding "self produced" value to a shopping experience of a full immersion type (Pine, Gilmore, 2000).

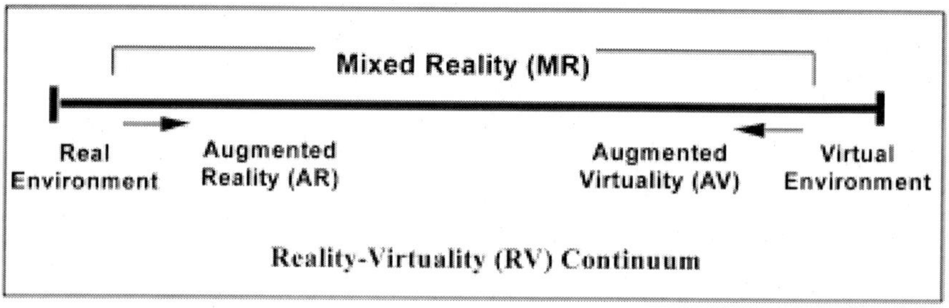

Figure 3. Milgram's reality.

Evident output defines this model of interactive and participant marketing – based on the contribution of the community of reference, decreeing obsolete the centrality of mass media in communications of product/brand – and redesigning the strategic interest surrounding the creation of interactive and social experience thus conferring on the product greater value (Mardegan et al., 2012) and increasing the brand equity.

In any event, while in inbound mobility (towards the subject) firms continue to hold a pre-eminent role, predisposing and guiding the subject-context interaction process, as concerns the outbound transfer, the control of mass media communication content by an ever growing number of actors widespread in spatial terms and/or close knit in virtual communities has become the norm – human broadcasters (Riva, 2012). Thus the confines of customer experience are redefined and extended. Links (mobility), creation of multimedia content (above all photos and videos) by sharing opinions on the product, reviews and comments on specific content, the use of technology to reinforce the sense of belonging to the community of reference, characterizing the consumer-product relation for the "C Generation" (Rosen, Lara-Ruiz, 2015, p. 21). Notwithstanding, with reference to the shopping experience promoted by full immersion technologies generally, numerous studies highlight how convenience (Kim et al., 2007; Magura, 2003; Mahatanankoon et al., 2005), a sense of trust and security – linked to the hedonistic value that can be derived (Bauer et al., 2007; Kleijnen et al., 2007) – are still fundamental factors in using "augmented" services and related mobility (see figure 4).

Supported by technology, the connected consumer achieves his purchases through the stages of awareness, research, acquirement, fulfillment, loyalty, engaging with brands at any stage of the shopping journey (Deloitte, 2014, p. 8) and sharing his flexible and sophisticated experience.

In short, the creative force of both bottom-up (governed by firm or brand) and top-down (creation and sharing of multimedia content) thanks to a digital grammatical basis that guarantees interaction between the parties, transforms the subject-consumer:

- from *trier,* using augmented reality to test the augmented product before buying in augmented contexts in terms of quality, problem solving capacity and promise,
- to *buyer*, relying on the initial value proposition, contextualized experience, aggregation dynamics and at the same time, privacy and safety of transactions,
- to *advertiser*, thanks to human broadcasting communication which via social networking, participates in the creating and spreading of the brand story, spontaneously motivating and supporting (if results are satisfactory) other potential *triers-buyers-advertisers*, thus generating on the whole, added value experience and as a consequence, more sales for the firm (Cuomo et al., 2014).

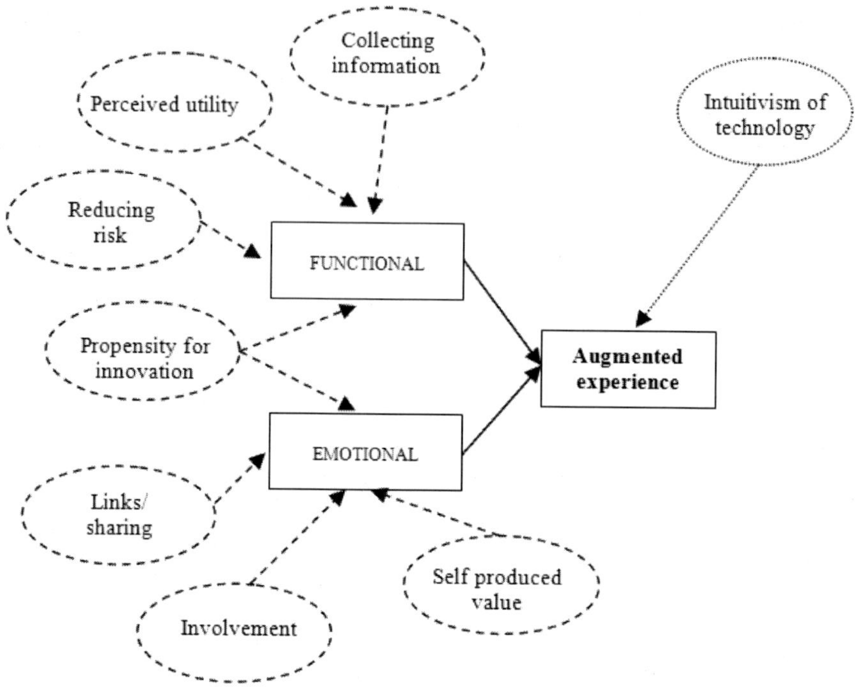

Figure 4. Factors influencing Augmented Experience.

Sure enough, from the firm point of view augmented reality strategies can support innovation and improve their return on investment (Figure 5).

As a consequence, organizations need to define key performance indicators and monitoring systems able to understand and measure the new context, considering that together with being connected, mobile, informed, ubiquitous, the consumer is especially "omnichannel"!

3. Augmented Experience in Store

Mobile augmented reality allows consumers to try on products in a social atmosphere, linking the application to e-commerce offers interesting opportunities.

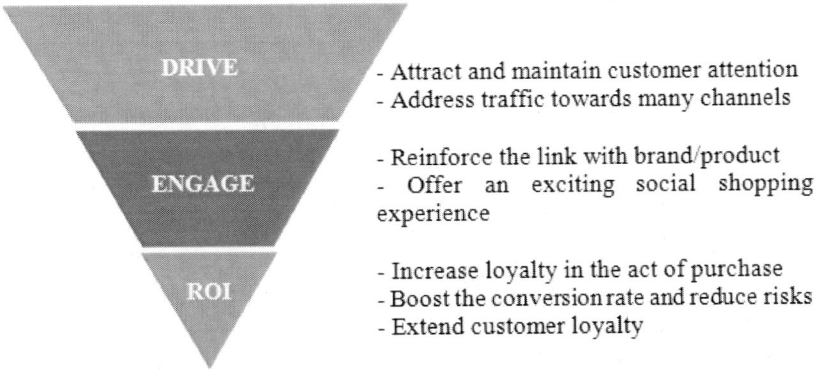

OnScreen Communication, 2014.

Figure 5. Innovation and ROI.

Optimization of local search, aggregation platforms and offer buildings and local referral marketing on social networks are the main areas to connect brick-and-mortar shopping experience with the benefits of digital channels (Heinemann, Gaiser, 2015a, p. 55). By engaging across different channels consumers can research and shop at their convenience, anytime, anywhere. Nevertheless, it is crucial presenting the right information in the right way, to effectively engage the augmented reality users without requiring them a high degree of cognitive effort (Ganapathy, 2013). This is true especially for smart natives, approaching the commercial landscape as customers and demanding such a professionalism, considering that in the next few years they will accelerate online, mobile and hybrid markets (Heinemann, Gaiser, 2015b, p. 2).

For instance, advanced technology for in-store shopping can be basically distinct between assisted shopping services and marketing-orientated services (Groß, 2015, pp. 228-232). In the first typology decision support systems are taken into consideration, based on the users' request for specific product attributes, i.e., retrieve data by scanning product barcodes or QR-codes with the mobile phone camera, by using special mobile shopping applications or by using an RFID-reader from the retailer; recommendation agent systems, providing meaningful recommendations that might be of consumers' interest; navigation systems (RFID-based and Wi-Fi based) helping users to reach any desired destination faster; mobile tracking systems, used to record consumers' shopping movements and time, giving retailers new insights into consumer behavior. The latter, marketing-orientated services, refer to mobile advertising or couponing, smart payments systems, rebates, loyalty cards and other location-based services, i.e., smart screens, trolleys with an integrated touch-screen through the aisle of a merchandise group, providing consumers with advertising information of the products in the aisle, and so on.

According to the technology acceptance model (TAM – Davis, 1989, 1993) and its contextualization in applying augmented reality in stores (Olson et al., 2012) the following elements are widely assumed to be the most relevant drivers of the user's acceptance and the intention to use the technology: perceived usefulness, as the ability to access relevant product information via augmented reality applications (apps); perceived ease of use, as the user-friendliness of the application; perceived enjoyment – as the extent to which the activity of using a technology "is perceived to be enjoyable in its own right" (Spreer, Kallweit, 2014, p. 21). Moreover, interacting with augmented reality through gesture controls seems to be promising from the users' perspective.

As a consequence of these technological and time changes in the contact between customer and goods/services, retailers need to modify their distributive strategies in order to accommodate today's fast-paced shoppers.

Purchases take place in new spaces, pending among digital and physical organization. Rather, the integration of the channels, both physical and digital, aims at realizing a single intuitive and integrated distribution system, firstly synthesized in the use of smart shopping carts and then of mobile devices and augmented solutions. Along with the objective of consumer behavior of going through cross-media and bridge-experiences, without interruption in shifting from one context to another, retailers' challenge consists in developing an integration that enriches the user experience.

Since markets are conversations (Levine et al., 2000), the "augmented talk" is truly the soul of selling, and retailers need to share with their customers this new code of dialogue.

Therefore, the concept of "customization" can be referred to the multi-channel consumer behavior, thus customizing a brand experience answers to their need for a total, ubiquitous and unconstrained access. Companies do not have to design multi-channel campaigns but multi-channel experiences, in which the physical shelves and the on-line catalogs merge.

Augmented reality is suitable for solving the problem of displaying multimedia content in retailing (Guven et al., 2009; Rashid et al., 2014) and also to tap segments that were previously not completely reachable through other marketing approaches (Shanthi, 2015, p. 65).

In effect the "augmented consumers", stimulated by technology, expert, independent and faster in their decision process, don't divert completely their interest in mobile devices even in shops. Hence, to meet this need the customer treatment in store becomes hybrid, thanks to video devices, touch screens, totems able to catch customers' attention and brighten up the atmosphere. In other words, the augmented retailing becomes more accessible, dynamic, amplified and even simplified in its digital use.

By this way consumers appropriate the servicescape, transforming it into a social and symbolic place, experiencing and interacting with other customers, in-store staff and visitors. The technological advancements, i.e., the introduction of analogical elements (sound recognition, computer vision) in the digital world and the creation of inter-connecting reality in the digital world, semantic analysis and concision of available information in the real world, and the proliferating of applications with easily adaptable interfaces, signify end services ever more specialized and customized (Frà et al., 2011). As it happens surfing in the web, the potential shopper, encouraged by fun activities and interaction with others (i.e., debates on forums, comments on social networks, gaming, apps, etc.) leaves his "marks" in the store (i.e., current position, shopping list, historical shopping, browsing behavior, as keywords for product search or web site views, preference on promotion offers, advertisements, and product attributes, etc.) valuable for customer profiling and better customer relationship.

In recent years firms planned and carried out field tests of augmented retailing, inserting smart signs in the point of purchase, with a melting pot of both materic and hyper technological elements, visual storytelling that overcome the product/brand description, to create augmented spaces supported by sophisticated systems of sound, pictures, lights (Zaghi, 2014, p. 84).

The following examples are considered more representative in changing the way clients perceive and consume retail (www.businessinsider.com).

In the cases shown augmented reality allows consumers to explore and experience products in safe environments, actively interacting with virtual objects, reducing risks and enhancing meaning. Users' perceived interactivity and compatibility are influential antecedents that shape their affective involvement with mobile retail apps, which in turn influences their intention to download and use mobile retail apps.

Some studies observe that the influence of affective involvement on purchase intention is more suitable than cognitive involvement (Kang et al., 2015).

Nevertheless, consumers perceive and acquire value by participating with and actively controlling objects and environments rather than merely reactively appreciating and evaluating online content.

Table 3. 51 Companies that are changing the way we shop

Concept	Retail
taking humans out of stores	Hointer (Seattle, Washington) - Year founded: 2012 Hointer is changing the way customers shop for clothes by using a robotic sales staff. Customers download an app, go to the showroom, and scan the QR codes of the clothing they'd like to try. The clothes are delivered automatically right to the fitting room, customers swipe their card on the tablet, and walk out.
trailblazing in simulated reality	Augment (Paris, France) - Year founded: 2010 Augment creates instant 3D models of products people want to buy and helps them determine if it's what they really want. It's currently working to provide simulations on customers' smartphones, making it possible to explore and buy products anywhere.
interactive an physical experiences	Story (Manhattan, New York) - Year founded: 2011 Story is a retail space that completely changes every four to eight weeks and gives e-commerce sites like Birchbox a physical store. Story began as "A Startup Store" in 2011. The business model is the first of its kind, not only because of how it brings e-commerce to life, but because Story includes paid brand partners who "sponsor" different iterations.
high-tech lab	Walmart (Bentonville, Arkansas) - Year founded: 1962 The world's largest retailer can't afford to let up. @WalmartLabs, its innovation center, exists to create the "core technology" that will blast Walmart into the future. Here, they're working on everything from specialized search engines to tracking buyers' habits to distribution solutions.
consumer preferences	OpenSky (Manhattan, New York) - Year founded: 2009 OpenSky.com is a social network with 2.5 million members for shopping that helps people discover, buy and share unique goods that match their individual taste. Members create their own shopping circle by connecting to their friends and choice of the site's industry insiders like Bobby Flay or Martha Stewart to create a personalized shopping experience and gain access to exclusive information, advice and product recommendations from people they trust.

Concept	Retail
personal experience	Shopkick (Palo Alto, California) - Year founded: 2010 Shopkick is a mobile app that sends shoppers rewards when they're at retailers like Crate & Barrel, Target and Old Navy and is easier than carrying loyalty cards. "No plastic cards, no confusing rules, no extra steps" Shopkick says on its website. Just walking in with a smart phone earns perks.
keep track of customers' purchases	Stylitics (Manhattan, New York) - Year founded: 2011 Stylitics is an app that logs what customers own, and keeps track of what they buy and wear. Ultimately, Stylitics tracks what brands customers wear the most and affirms which companies they're most loyal to.
showrooming an asset	Restoration Hardware (Corte Madera, California) - Year founded: 1979 Restoration Hardware decreased its number of physical stores and used the remaining ones as showrooms. Sofas, tables, rugs and other decor were meticulously arranged with an emphasis on the aesthetic. Customers could find even more merchandise online or in catalogs while shopping in the stores.
Loyalty programs	Target (Minneapolis, Minnesota) - Year founded: 1902 Target's REDcard is one of the most attractive, simple loyalty cards among the big every-day retailers. Between the 5 percent discount, no annual fee, and additional perks, the card is making a difference for consumers (who pay their balances on time).
Personalizing the customer experience	Knot Standard (Manhattan, New York) - Year founded: 2010 Knot Standard takes the anxiety out of shopping for men by offering local tailors who provide measurements and online ordering of suits. The result is a better-fitting product and happier customer.
Staying ahead	Macy's (Cincinnati, Ohio) - Year founded: 1858 Macy's continues to identify and act on new retail trends, coming up with great new ideas. Beauty Spot, for instance, is a cosmetics concept kiosks to improve the experience on the selling floor. It's also making strides with location tracking in its big stores, delivery systems, and digital receipt.
The look of stores	JCPenney (Plano, Texas) - Year founded: 1902 The company would cease promotions, wagering the in-store experience. The full store of branded shops, a half-mile long aisle for customers to hang out, and a seasonal entertainment area have the potential to change how people buy in department stores.

This interactive shopping experience creates active experiential values, enriching consumer ROI (including returns on financial, time, behavioral, and mental investments that consumers made to acquire rewards and benefits - Huang, Liu, 2014).

In synthesis, in order to survive, nowadays retailing has to adopt a multichannel approach, even omnichannel, in which firms are called to think digital, trigging a process of cultural evolution and upgrading of skills involving the organization in its whole. It is crucial to draw a single customer experience, integrating online and in-store interactions through multiple touch points: pick-up in-store, online visibility on stock available in store, integrated customer care, reserved apps, RFID/QR code, smart mirrors, and so on, to access digital content in-store are just a few examples. Finally, connection with users has to be constantly active through listening, interaction and sharing of quality content that can excite, inform and educate their followers. Social networks can be useful to reach this aim, providing that they have been inserted in the marketing strategy. Upstream of this, retailers have to invest in analytics and monitoring augmented reality events and efforts: the adoption of these systems is ultimately critical to effectively connect with their users/customers. Profiling and supervising their behavior both in physical and digital places, attending them before, during and after the purchasing process allows retailers to quickly intercept opportunities and accurately respond to customers' expectations.

4. Some Critical Considerations

As it appears in recent analysis, augmented reality seems to suggest a strategic/operative marketing approach able to develop new opportunities for businesses, encouraging the contact between firms and users and inducing a physiological growth of attendance and attention in the stores. Despite this, it is not immune from problems and limitations.

Focusing on its application, it is evident that the potentialities of augmented reality are still limited by the "reef" of the degree of diffusion and usability of devices and tools, which do not allow a totally effective and intelligent use. Thus at the moment augmented reality seems to be relegated to a role of reading and returning overlapping data.

Besides, there are psychological and relational pitfalls.

Deeply observing the phenomenon of in-store augmented reality, it emerges a "full-load" dimension where additional information, animations, details, technical deepening etc. could easily cause an "information chaos" for the consumer, that is confusion and disorientation resulting in a potential distortion of the brand/consumer connection. Indeed the traditional role of the brand – quality standard guarantee and indicator and purchasing process simplifier in the real environment – does not easily active in the augmented reality environment because of information overflow and of users inadequacy/difficulty to select really useful information. Augmented reality applications, therefore, could be counter-productive because they make more muddled, or in some cases impossible, the selection of useful data to the decision making. This might cause a feeling of stress (Gay-Lussac, 2012) in users resulting in a decisional paralysis, that is inability to select in the alternatives for excessive presence of elements and information, often equivalent, that produce disorientation or even cognitive dissonance.

On the contrary, it creates a value experience, however, if augmented reality simplifies – in terms of decision-making – the user experience by giving them immediate benefits, identifiable, ensuring an easy use of devices, despite their technological limits (Prunesti, Lalli, 2011). By this way it can spontaneously create new interactions between people and "things" (whether real or virtual) and dyadic value.

Thus, it would be necessary to structure the "in-store augmented experience" identifying factors really able to capture the customer, as well as to provide those necessary, effective and helpers shopping experience information contents, even sometimes removing additional information, which can result redundant. Despite the lexical antithesis, "diminished reality" can be considered a form of augmented reality, too (Cuomo et al., 2014). In some circumstances, in fact, decreasing the dose of information conveyed (Enomoto, Saito, 2007; Herling, Broll, 2010) might even facilitate decision making and therefore the purchase. If for a purchase problematic and complex (as is the case eg for the goods to purchase weighted or special assets) the augmented reality is strongly effective for other types – i.e., impulse purchases – instead, it might be preferable a "diminished reality" that does not influence potential consumers negatively (creating an overload of elements).

On the side of the information system, augmented reality promotes in-store interactions motivating the "feedbacks generation", users virtually in contact with other visitors or potential clients releasing valuable information to the company, which allows to better understand their needs. Indeed the indications obtained are indirectly influenced and oriented by the same firm/brand that, drawing the structure of the in-store experience, influences exchanges and, therefore, the type of information exchanged (even if bottom-up).

From the point of view of the user, instead, it should be remembered that everyone has a personal inclination for technology knowledge and devices use, generating a multitude of different perceptions and in-store experiences. In fact, a visitor with a high inclination/knowledge toward augmented reality technologies will not be conquered by a store with a trivial and not challenging augmented reality experience. Therefore, this user does not receive any kind of additional element and incentive to stay in the store and buy, with the resulting in a value destruction. Conversely, a user not interested in virtual reality and unskilled in the use of new technologies could feel disoriented and inadequate in a store offering strong augmented experiences, to the point of trying a strong aversion towards the point of selling, destroying resources and value.

In the sum, the store could be structured to catalyze interactions between users with different levels of technological skills and psychological needs, reinforcing the aggregation of an heterogeneous "tribe" around the brand. For a correct and more complete profiling of the customer system it should considered also their "need for control" on situations, which is one of the primary motivations of the human acting (Vannucci, 2012).

The marketing literature refers to this line of study that interprets the consumer as an individual who, among the different areas of life, also expresses that of consumption, paying particular attention to the psychological component in the determination of buying behavior; from this, the causal relationship between the stimulus from the external environment (increased/decreased reality of the store), the affective/cognitive structure of individuals (low/high info eager) and the resulting behavior may become the subject of discussion to understand the link between augmented reality and use of the area retail by the consumer.

Moving from these considerations, it is necessary to reflect on the opportunity and the way to realize an in-store augmented experience, with regards to technical and operational aspects.

In addition, it should not be underestimate the phenomenon of showrooming, the tendency of users to experience the store just as a place to learn more about the offer but not where to make purchase, sometimes encouraged by augmented reality, too. Although ROPO – research online and purchase offline - is today a widespread tendency, retailers have to not underestimate the warning signals above described, conveying the purchasing in store more involving, convenient, enjoyable, riskless, or in other words of greater value for their customers.

In conclusion, retailers should consider the augmented reality as a "project" for value creation – and not only as a marketing tool – to integrate harmoniously into a more broad and complex brand's overall customer marketing ecosystem, where genius, technology and content must bring together traditional and innovative forms, and related instruments, to generate effective customer engagement. Hence, to avoid the risk of giving in to the technophobia, without considering actual earnings both for customers and firms, it is necessary to constantly draw towards a breakable balance among a communication-interaction and a communication-meaning, where customers arbitrate with their purchase, satisfaction, perhaps loyalty.

REFERENCES

Atzuma, R. T. (1997). A Survey of Augmented Reality. *Presence,* 6 (4): 355-385.

Brognara, R. (2014). Rivoluzione mobile. I cambiamenti sociali e di marketing prodotti dalle tecnologie mobili. Franco Angeli, Milano.

Caudell, T. P., Mitzell, D. W. (1992). Augmented reality: an application of heads-up display technology to manual manufacturing processes. *System Sciences,* 2, 659-669.

Cuomo, M. T., Metallo, G., Tortora, D., Testa, M., Kitchen, P. J. (2009). Building brand equity: the genetic coding of Mediterranea brands. *Euromed. Journal of Business*, 4, 3, 237-253.

Cuomo, M. T., Tortora, D., Metallo, G. (2014). In Store Augmented Reality: Retailing Strategies for Smart Communities. *Mondo Digitale*, 49, 1-12.

Davis, F. D. (1989). Perceived usefulness, perceived ease of use, and user acceptance of information technology. *MIS quarterly*, 13 (3): 319-340.

Davis, F. D. (1993). User acceptance of information technology: system characteristics, user perceptions and behavioral impacts. *International Journal of Man-Machine Studies,* 38 (3): 475-487.

Deloitte (2014). The omnichannel opportunity. Unlocking the power of the connected consumer. A report for eBay, http://www2.deloitte.com

Enomoto, A., Saito, H. (2007). Diminished reality using multiple handheld cameras. *Proc. ACCV*, 7, 130-135.

Frà, C., Lamorte, L., Martini, G. (2011). Dall'augmented reality al check-in. *Notiziario tecnico Telecom. Italia*, 3, 20-31.

Ganapathy, S. (2013). Design guidelines for mobile augmented reality: User experience Weidong Huang, W., Alem, L., Livingston, M. A. (editors),

Human Factors in Augmented Reality Environments, Springer, New York.

Gay-Lussac, M., Pour vivre heureux, vivons sans infos? (2012). *Le Cercle Psy,* 4, 7.

Groß, M. (2015),Mobile shopping: a classification framework and literature review. *International Journal of Retail and Distribution Management*, 43 (3): 221-241.

Guven, S., Oda, O., Podlaseck, M., Stavropoulos, H., Kolluri, S., Pingali, G. (2009). Social mobile augmented reality for retail. Proceedings of the International Conference on Pervasive Computing and Communications (PerCom 2009): 1-3.

Heinemann, G., Gaiser, C. (2015, a). "Always on and Always in Touch": The New Buying Behaviour, 1-12. In: Heinemann, G., Gaiser, C. (eds). Social – Local – Mobile. The Future of Location-based Services. Springer Berlin Heidelberg.

Heinemann, G., Gaiser, C. (2015, b). Location-based services as Base Factor No. 2 for SoLoMo, 55-99. In: Heinemann, G., Gaiser, C. (eds). Social – Local – Mobile. The Future of Location-based Services. Springer Berlin Heidelberg.

Herling, J., Broll, W. (2010). Advanced Self-contained Object Removal for Realizing Real-time Diminished Reality in Unconstrained Environments, IEEE International Symposium on Mixed and Augmented Reality, *Science and Technology Proceedings*, October 13-16, Seoul, Korea, 207-212.

Hoffman, D. L., Novak, T. P. (2012). Toward a deeper understanding of social media. *Journal of Interactive Marketing*, 26 (2), 69-70.

http://arblog.inglobetechnologies.com, accessed March, 10 2015.

http://businessinsider.com/companies-revolutionizing-retail-2013-2?op=1&IR= T#ixzz3VIU3gaB2, accessed March, 20 2015.

http://visualistan.com/2014/07/augmented-reality-facts-and-figures.html, accessed March, 13 2015.

Huang, T.-L. H., Liu, F. (2014). Formation of augmented-reality interactive technology's persuasive effects from the perspective of experiential value. *Internet Research*, 24 (1): 82-109.

International Data Corporation (2015). Worldwide Quarterly Smart Connected Device Tracker, March 20, 2015, www.idc.com.

Kang, J.-Y. M., Mee Mun, J., Johnson, K. K. P. (2015). In-store mobile usage: Downloading and usage intention toward mobile location-based retail apps. *Computers in Human Behavior*, 46: 210–217.

Kim, H., Chan, H. C., Gupta, S. (2007). Value-based adoption of mobile internet: An empirical investigation. *Decision Support Systems*, 43 (1): 111-126.

Kleijnen, M., Ruyter, K., Wetzels, M. (2007). An assessment of value creation in mobile service delivery and the moderating role of time consciousness. *Journal of Retailing*, 83 (1): 33-46.

Levine, R., Locke, C., Searls, D., Weinberger, D. (2000). The cluetrain manifesto: The end of business as usual. *New York Times Book Review,* 105 (13), 17-18.

Lundqvist, A., Liljander, V., Gummerus, J. (2013), The impact of storytelling on the consumer brand experience: The case of a firm-originated story. *Journal of Brand Management*, 20, 4, 283-297.

Magura, B. (2003). What hooks m-commerce customers? *MIT Sloan Management Review,* 44 (3): 9-16.

Mahatanankoon, P. (2005). Wen, H. J., Lim, B., Consumer-based m-commerce: exploring consumer perception of mobile applications. *Computer Standards and Interfaces*, 27 (4): 347-357.

Mardegan, P., Riva, G., Pettiti, M. (2012). Mobile Marketing: la pubblicità in tasca, Lupetti Editore, Bologna.

Milgram, P., Takemura, H., Utsumi, A., F. Kishino, F. (1994). Augmented reality: A class of displays on the reality-virtuality continuum. *Telemanipulator and Telepresence Technologies*, 2351, 282-292.

Olsson, T., Kärkkäinen, T., Lagerstam, E., Ventä-Olkkonen, L. (2012). User evaluation of mobile augmented reality scenarios. *Journal of Ambient Intelligence and Smart Environments,* 4 (1): 29-47.

OnScreen Communication (2014). Home & Luxury: nuove tecnologie per il retail. www.onscreencommunication.it

Pine, J. B. I. I., Gilmore, J. H. (2000). L'economia delle esperienze. Oltre il sevizio, Etas, Milano.

Prunesti, A., Lalli, F. (2011). Geolocalizzazione e mobile marketing. Fare business con le App e i social game, Franco Angeli, Milano.

Raajan, N. R., Vinodhini, A., Vidhyalakshmi, N. (2013). Augmented reality based assistance. *International Journal of Engineering and Technology (IJET),* 5 (2), 1652-1657.

Rashid, Z., Morenza-Cinos, M., Pous, R., Melià-Seguí, J. (2014). Mobile augmented reality for browsing physical spaces. Proceedings of the 2014 ACM International Joint Conference on Pervasive and Ubiquitous Computing, *ACM,* 2014: 155-158.

Rosen, L. D., Lara- Ruiz, J. M. (2015). Workplace, Personal, and Technology- Related Values, Beliefs, and Attitudes Across Five Generations of Americans. The Wiley Blackwell Handbook of Psychology, Technology and Society, 20.

Scatena, S., Mardegan, P. (2012). Mobile Marketing: stato dell'arte e applicazioni pratiche. *Micro and Macro Marketing*, 2, 219-235.

Schultz, D. E., Block, M. P. (2011). Understanding customer brand engagement behaviors in today's interactive marketplace. *Micro and Macro Marketing,* 2, 227-244.

Shanthi, R. (2015). The Impact of Augmented Reality on E-Commerce. *Journal of Marketing and Consumer Research*, 8: 64-73.

Spreer, P., Kallweit, K. (2014). Augmented Reality in Retail: Assessing the Acceptance and Potential for Multimedia Product Presentation at the PoS. *SOP Transactions on Marketing Research*, 1 (1): 23-31.

Trubow, M. (2011). Sales technology: selling with augmented reality. Hidden Creative Ltd, www.hiddenltd.com, September 5, 1-14.

Trubow, M. (2013). What is Augmented reality? An infographic for sales and marketing professional.Hidden Creative Ltd, www.hiddenltd.com, January 28.

Vannucci, M. (2012). Le incertezze della mente. Fra perdita di controllo e meccanismi compensatori. *Psicologia contemporanea*, settembre/ottobre, 44-49.

Varnali, K., Toker, A. (2010). Mobile marketing research: The-state-of-the-art. *International Journal of Information Management*, 30, 144-151.

Venkatesh, R. (2015). Mobile Marketing – From Marketing Strategy to Mobile Marketing Campaign Implementation. *International Journal of Research,* 2 (2): 1175-1187.

Zaghi, K. (2014). Visual merchandising. Orientamenti e paradigmi della comunicazione del punto vendita. FrancoAngeli, Milano.

In: Augmented REality
Editor: Raymond Hughes

ISBN: 978-1-63482-902-1

Chapter 5

Augmented Reality for Cultural Heritage Using Vision-based User Tracking: A Fusion Approach

***Erkan Bostanci*[1,*], *Nadia Kanwal*[2,†] *and Adrian F. Clark*[3,‡]**
[1]Ankara University, Ankara, Turkey
[2]Lahore College for Women University, Lahore, Pakistan
[3]University of Essex, Colchester, UK

Abstract

Augmented Reality (AR) provides an entertaining means for displaying 3D reconstructions of ancient buildings *in situ* for cultural heritage. Finding the pose, position and orientation, of the user is crucial for such applications since this information will be used to define the viewpoint that will be used for rendering the models. Images acquired from a camera can be used as the background for such augmentations. To make the most out of this available information, these images can also be utilized to find a pose estimate. This paper presents contributions for vision-based methods for estimating the pose of the user in both indoor and outdoor environments. Keyframe-based tracking algorithm is presented. Continuing with vision-based approaches, Kinect sensor was also used to find the pose of a user for *in situ* augmentations making use of the natural features

*E-mail address: ebostanci@ankara.edu.tr
†E-mail address: nadia.kanwal@lcwu.edu.pk
‡E-mail address: alien@essex.ac.uk

in the environment. Skeleton-tracking was also found to be beneficial for such applications. The paper then investigates combining the vision-based estimates with measurements from other sensors, GPS and IMU, in order to improve the tracking accuracy in outdoor environments. Finally, several AR applications are presented that make use of these methods. The first one is for *in situ* augmentation for displaying historical columns and augmenting users, the second is a virtual visit to an ancient building and the third is a game which can also be played inside the augmentation of the building in the second application.

Keywords: user tracking, computer vision, augmented reality, sensor fusion

AMS Subject Classification: 68U05, 68T45, 68U01

1. Introduction

Technologies presented every day have brought us into a state of mind which is more demanding and more difficult to satisfy. We cannot be satisfied with the things we have, we do and, more recently, we see! Our eyes look for additional content in the same environment we see every day. This demand provides a powerful input to research as new challenges to be addressed and unknown areas to be investigated. As new solutions for existing problems are developed and as researchers share their future prospects with public, the demand is even more increased because the results will be combined with the future dreams of people, forming a cycle.

AR is a technology which attempts to fulfil the demand for additional content in everyday scenes by inserting virtual (usually synthetic, though live videos can also be inserted) objects over the content we would normally see, in the form of overlays, typically using a head-mounted display (HMD). Having a wide spectrum of application areas, ranging from industrial maintenance and repair tasks to military training and entertainment, AR has already shown that it has much potential.

This research concentrates on AR for cultural heritage. The principal reason for performing AR reconstructions in cultural heritage is that the owners of sites are usually reticent to permit physical reconstructions *in situ* so that the archaeology remains undisturbed for future generations. Developments in multimedia technology facilitate the learning experience in cultural heritage with the aid of improved user interaction methods. Developed models (*e.g.*, Figure 1) or virtual tours of reconstructions of archaeological sites provide entertaining means of learning.

(a) Temple in ruins (b) A reconstruction from [1, 2] (c) 3D model based on (a) and (b)

Figure 1. Views from the Hadrian Temple in Ephesus, Turkey.

However, *ex situ* reconstructions such as models and movies [3, 4] are difficult to visualize in the context of the archaeological remains. AR reconstructions can be produced *in situ* with minimal physical disturbance, an attractive property, even though they may take a significant time to develop due to a number of challenges.

An important challenge is producing a realistic output image in which the inserted objects are coherent with the real-world scene. Locating and tracking the user accurately in the environment [5] is key to this process since the user position and orientation determine the perspective information required for augmenting the scene. The process of tracking the user position is relatively easy if the user stands in a fixed, known position in a structured environment, looking at a fixed scene. Tracking the user becomes much more difficult if he or she is able to move freely in an outdoor environment where there is no limit for possible movements. Here, we will show that this is best achieved using a combination of position and orientation estimates from several sensors, using efficient algorithms to perform user tracking in real-time.

The main focus of this paper is on finding the position of the user since this is a crucial part for such a system. This will be handled using a tracking system that comprises a camera, a GPS receiver and an IMU. Each of the sensors are low cost and public grade, in other words the accuracy of the sensors are not satisfactory for the application when they are used alone. For this reason, sensor fusion will be implemented to achieve more accurate position and orientation estimates.

The camera used in the system has a the task of acquiring images of the scene, which will be used for two purposes. Firstly, they will be used by the vision-based algorithm developed in order to provide estimates for the user position using algorithms from the computer vision domain. The literature provides many different methods for vision-based pose estimation and we makes use of some of these methods with a novel approach. Secondly, the images will be used to produce the final output where augmentations can be overlaid on the original scene.

The GPS receiver and IMU will aid the camera for positional estimates since the prototype system is intended to be used outdoors. Positional estimates from these sensors will be unified with the vision-based ones in order to produce more accurate results. A second task for the IMU is to provide orientation estimates using a recent robust method from the literature [6]. Use of Microsoft's Kinect sensor was also investigated for producing *in situ* augmentations for historical columns, and skeleton-tracking features for augmenting participants of the system.

The rest of the paper is structured as follows: Section 2 presents current problems with tracking systems. The tracking methods presented here are given in Section 3 followed by Section 4 where different AR applications are presented. Finally, the paper is concluded with future directions in Section 5.

2. Related Work

Tracking, the process of locating a user in an environment, is critical to the accuracy of AR applications as more realistic results are obtained in the presence of accurate AR registration [5]. This process includes determining the position and orientation of the AR user.

Generally, the most important part is tracking the head, as the user typically wears a AR on which the augmented images of the real world are displayed. Furthermore, a tracking system mounted on the head has better signal reception if GPS will be used, has a good field of view (FOV) of the scene for visual tracking, and removes the need for lever-arm compensation (*i.e.,* adjusting the reference frames of the tracking system to align with the user's eyes).

The improved accuracy of an AR system due to tracking also prevents problems such as visual capture [7] and does not allow visual sensors to gain priority over other sensors. For instance, inadequate registration accuracy can cause the user to reach or walk to the wrong part of the real environment because the augmentation has been displayed on another part. The eyes of the users get used to the error in the virtual environment and after some time of usage they start to accept these errors as correct, which is not desirable.

Current tracking systems still have many problems. Two types of errors were defined in [7], namely static and dynamic errors. Before giving details about problems when using different types of sensors, these two important terms will be explained.

The errors in tracking systems are considered as static errors due to the inadequate accuracy provided by current systems. Dynamic errors are due to delays. The end-to-end system delay is the time elapsed between the time when the tracking system measures the position and orientation of the user to the time when the images appear on the display.

All of the studies given in [5] are able to present good results in terms of both tracking accuracy and application domains. However, they work well only in a small environment such as a room corner [8], a desktop [9] or a whole room [10] — all indoor environments. In [11], localization was performed according to known 3D junctions and AR tests were carried out with a rectangular pattern visible in the view during processing. The system used tokens as markers in [12], although markerless tracking was claimed.

Conversely, this research will be directed towards the use of AR in outdoor environments. There are important differences between indoor and outdoor environments for vision-based tracking methods. First of all, indoor environments are generally limited in terms of location, and hence are more predictable. Fewer features are required for tracking. Second, the lighting (which is a very important factor for vision-based processing) is constant for an indoor environment, where this may vary largely due to the clouds, shades, *etc*. Lower contrast also poses a challenge for finding and tracking robust features. Another important factor to consider is the distance for acquiring the depth information. When a feature lies closer to the camera, the camera can extract depth information after a small movement via computational stereo. However, when the feature is far from the camera, a large camera motion is required to estimate its depth. Finally, outdoor applications do not allow placing markers; natural features must be extracted for tracking.

Vision methods allow both tracking and managing residual errors. They are low cost. The problem with these methods is the lack of robustness [13]. For some applications (*e.g.*, [14]), there may be a great probability of incorrect matches since the texture of the ground is mostly similar in different areas. It was stated in [13] that the structure of AR models is more difficult than VR since the former uses geometry not only for visualization but also for occlusion handling and vision-based tracking of scene features.

Also for visual tracking, the features to be used as landmarks should be invariant to changes in lighting and viewpoint. Since this is not always possible, vision-based tracking for outdoor environments is reported to be fragile [15]. Using a camera as the only sensor was found to be accurate but expensive in computation [16].

SFM methods use off-line batch processing methods [17, 18] on video sequences. The 3D structure of the environment can then be extracted using non-linear minimization techniques (*e.g.,* bundle adjustment). These off-line methods cannot provide the real-time performance [19] required for AR. Therefore a sequential method which performs the localization [20] will be more useful.

Standard GPS has an error of the order of 10m. However, it improves when a differential GPS or real-time kinematic correction is used. Line of sight can be a problem for the satellites in urban environments [21] or under dense tree canopy [22]. Other problems with GPS were explained in detail in [23]. The system developed in [24] reported tracking problems occurring when GPS was used as the only sensor, and the authors suggested using sensor fusion or GPS dead-reckoning.

Double integration of data from inertial trackers cause drift errors to propagate rapidly [14]. Active tracking systems require calibrated sensors and signal sources in a prepared environment and tracking equipment can be affected by signal noise, degradation with distance and interference sources [25]. Magnetic trackers can be interfered by the ferro-magnetic objects in the environment [26]. A system with gyroscopes and accelerometers provide good bandwidth; however, it is prone to integrated errors and long term stability is not guaranteed [27].

There are several issues that must be considered for an accurate system. As with almost all other vision-based systems, incorrect feature correspondences pose a problem since low precision and recall rates were reported for feature matching with images [28]. For a vision-based approach, RANSAC [29] is useful for the data association problem but it was reported to result in incorrect estimates occasionally [30]. SIFT or SURF descriptors are considered as an important barrier to achieve full frame-rate operation [31]. However, using these robust descriptors can help solve the problems described above.

Similar problems come into consideration in the SLAM systems used in robotics. First of all, data association, finding a unique correspondence between the feature model and the observation due to incorrect correspondences mentioned above is a problem. The second problem is linearisation due to the characteristics of current SLAM methods (*e.g.,* Kalman Filtering, KF). Linearisation problems affect both the filter stability and convergence resulting in less accurate localization [32].

SLAM applications on robots usually have odometry sensors, providing speed information which is used as a control parameter in a filtering approach. This information is not available for a moving person and the movements of the person cannot be controlled like a robot. The system in [33] generates motion commands to maximize the accuracy of a SLAM application. A better method is to use an inertial sensor to decide on the motion model in a multiple model approach like [34]. Also, modest speeds are given for a robot as 1m/s [35]. This speed is almost the same for a tourist walking in an archaeological site to examine the ruins.

A vision-based approach is promising for motion estimation. Some of the previous systems [25, 36, 37] have used methods that employ computer vision methods for tracking; however, these systems are aimed for users standing at a fixed position. For a user in motion, most methods use GPS and inertial trackers for this purpose [38, 39, 24, 40].

Recently, Oskiper *et al.* [41] developed a tightly-coupled EKF visual–inertial tracking system for AR for outdoor environments using a relatively expensive sensor (XSens, MTi-G). The system used feature-level tracking in each frame and measurements from the GPS in order to reduce drift. In addition to this, a digital elevation map of the environment was used as well as a pre-built landmark database for tracking in indoor environments where GPS reception is not available (although it was claimed that no assumption about the environment was made).

The idea of using different sensors together is quite useful because different sensors can counteract each other's weaknesses and provide more accuracy. Inertial sensors can be used for stability and robustness in cases of rapid motion or occlusion [16]. Even better results can be obtained with a similar approach as [42] by fusing GPS measurements with measurements obtained from vision system. Tracking accuracy and convergence speed is claimed to improve by using more sensors [43].

3. Tracking Methods

This section presents 3 different vision-based tracking methods. The first method uses a single camera to estimate the user motion. This estimation is aided with measurements from a GPS and IMU in the second method. The third method uses the Kinect sensor in order to find the camera pose using natural features already available in the scene in addition to employing Kinect's skeleton tracking features to track users in the environment.

3.1. Keyframe Based Motion Estimation

This approach uses keyframes to estimate the camera motion using two-view geometry, using a combination of the methods proposed in [18], [44, 45], and [46]. Geiger *et al.* [47] proposed dense 3D reconstruction and visual odometry, using the approach described in [44] and [45], for stereo motion estimation and tracking autonomous cars. This approach also used a KF to refine the initial estimate obtained from the stereo approach for noise removal.

Instead of taking a direction that uses dense reconstruction as in [47], the method described here uses keyframes selected following the approach of [18, 46] where Royer *et al.* used PNP on features detected from the keyframes. The approach used in this section is slightly modified since the original method can skip too many frames, which would allow the system to miss some important movements.

The method proposed here uses keyframes acquired from a single camera aligned parallel to the direction of motion (as detailed in Section 3.1.1). Features extracted from these keyframes are used to estimate the motion of the camera using two-view geometry [45]. This motion estimate was applied to the previous position in order to obtain the new position estimate, a method similar to dead-reckoning [48] where the current position of the user is deduced based on the previous position and the motion in between.

Following the approach of [47], a KF was used to refine the visual estimate initially; however this filtering part was removed later since the vision system was to be used in conjunction with other sensors (*i.e.*, GPS and IMU).

Details of the motion estimation method will be provided in the following sections after presenting the assumptions behind the system and an important challenge due to the alignment of the camera in the following subsection.

3.1.1. Assumptions and Challenges

Similar to other vision-based systems, the motion estimation method presented here depends on the following assumptions:

- Calibrated camera: The intrinsic parameters of the camera must be known since projections will use these parameters in order to triangulate features for motion estimation.
- Static environment: Objects in the surroundings are considered to be non-moving which is different from the work in [49] where tracking was performed on moving objects.
- Known starting point: The sequence starts from a known location (can be arbitrary, but should be defined as the starting point) due to the successive nature of finding position estimates (*i.e.,* dead-reckoning). This does not imply that a preprocessing step is required for the algorithm to run.

These assumptions describe an environment in which more robust results can be obtained. Before the keyframe based localization algorithm is explained, it is important to describe two challenges that were faced during the experiments due to the alignment of the camera according to the direction of motion, since this affects the accuracy of the estimation. When the camera is aligned perpendicular to the motion direction (*e.g.,* the SLAM system in [50]), the disparity of features in the environment can be better observed, allowing the reconstruction to be more accurate with smaller projection errors; as a result, the estimation of camera motion will be better. Furthermore, the alignment of the camera and the direction of motion also affects the feature matching results since changes in feature scales will not be the same in different configurations.

It is known that the result of triangulation is more accurate for objects that are close to the camera [51], as the camera requires little motion to observe these objects from different viewpoints. For objects that are further ahead, the accuracy of depth estimation degrades as the distance of the camera to the objects increases. This situation is illustrated in Figure 2 where two configurations are shown in a scene that includes three objects at different distances from the camera.

In the first configuration (Figure 2(a)), the direction of the camera is perpendicular to the motion direction. In this case, features from the nearby object

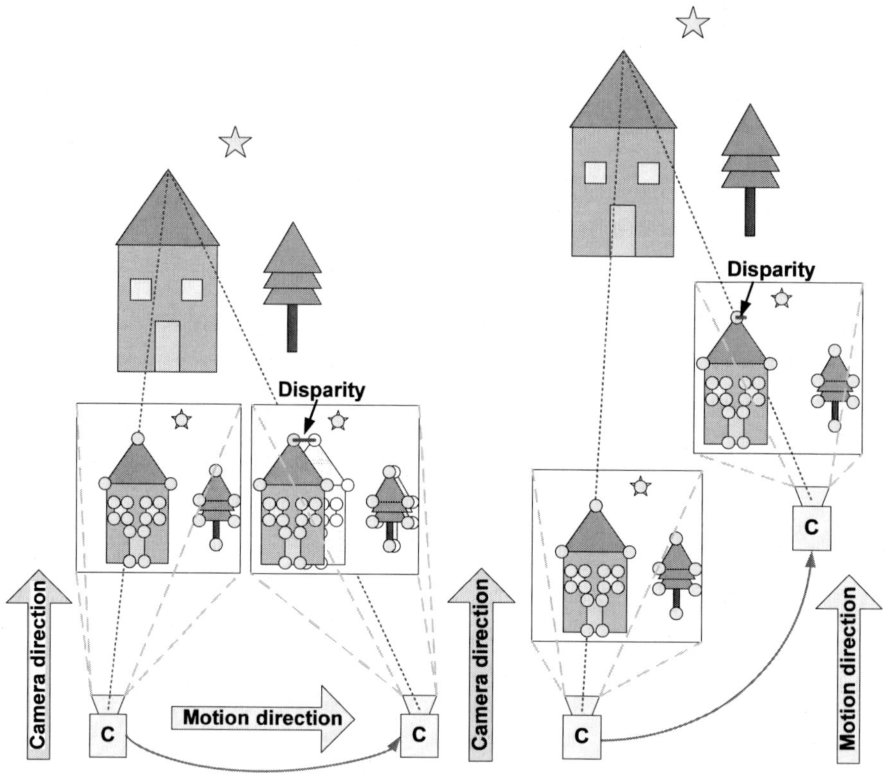

(a) Camera direction is perpendicular to the direction of motion.

(b) Directions of camera and motion are parallel to each other.

Figure 2. Alignment of the camera relative to the direction of motion. Of the three objects in the scene, the house is the closest object and the star is the furthest with the tree located between them. Second frames in both figures show the previous projected positions of the objects to demonstrate the difference. Notice how the disparities of these objects are changing in their image projections as the camera moves in different directions.

(house) have a larger disparity between the frames. Disparities from the tree are less significant, and there is no visible disparity in the feature from the star.

The challenge appears when the camera is pointing in the direction of motion as in Figure 2(b). In this configuration, the baseline shortens and it becomes more difficult to observe parallax, even for nearby objects, and this becomes almost impossible for objects residing further ahead.

A second challenge of using such a configuration is related to changes in feature scales. In a horizontal motion (*i.e.,* when the camera is not parallel to the direction of motion), the scales of features will not change much; rather, the changes will be in position. However, in a vertical type of motion as shown in Figure 2(b), feature scales will vary greatly. This situation poses a challenge for the feature descriptors, particularly for their scale-invariance properties. For this reason, descriptors that are used in the vision system should be able to accommodate such great changes in scale.

Despite the two challenges explained above, the second configuration was used in the experiments, because the images acquired by the camera are not only used for user tracking but also used as the background scene for the AR applications presented in Section 4. A setting with the former configuration would not allow this using only a single camera.

3.1.2. Extraction of Keyframes

When performing localization on a video sequence, it is useful to select a subset of the frames, a process known as keyframing. In this process, it is important to select these keyframes so that the number of feature correspondences between them is above some threshold. This allows the system to estimate estimate the motion correctly and not skip any important movement. Keyframing offer the following two benefits:

- Large baseline: The estimation of 3D structure is not accurate when the baseline is small (Figure 2) *i.e.,* there is not enough motion between the keyframes.
- Performance: The complete algorithm is run on a smaller set of images (using 40–60% of the frames in this case) instead of the complete sequence.

The keyframing approach described in the following paragraph is based on [18, 46]. In addition to their method, an extra heuristic was used to prevent skipping too many frames as this may result in missing any sudden motion that may have lasted for just a few frames.

The first image acquired by the camera, $frame_0$, is always selected as the first keyframe ($keyframe_0$). For the following frames, a set of feature correspondences were computed between the last keyframe $keyframe_n$ and each of following frames $frame_i$. Spurious matches are eliminated from this set using RANSAC. When the number of these correspondences falls below a threshold ($t = 400$, found experimentally), a new keyframe is extracted as $keyframe_{n+1}$. This selection mechanism is illustrated in Figure 3.

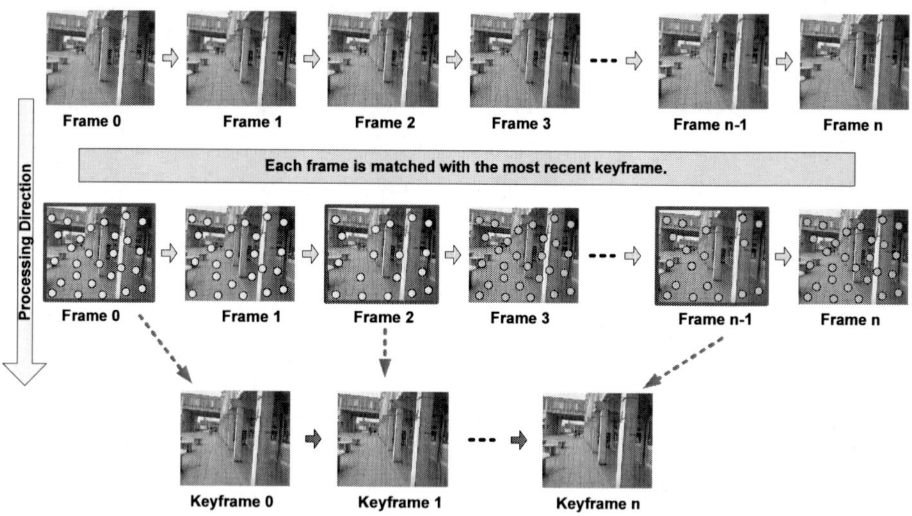

Figure 3. Selecting keyframes based on image correspondences. Coloured circles represent feature correspondences between frames acquired by the camera and the most recent keyframe. When the number of these correspondences fall below a threshold, a new keyframe is extracted and used for motion estimation.

After each keyframe is extracted, the number of skipped frames is counted, allowing at most 3 frames to be skipped. This method of extracting keyframes uses 40% – 60% of the frames, allowing better speed performance and providing a large enough baseline for the motion estimation. The next steps include finding possible solutions for the transformation between the most recent two keyframes and then selecting the most appropriate one.

3.1.3. Finding Possible Solutions

The localization of the camera is performed by using the essential matrix instead of using the fundamental matrix, making use of the calibration parameters [52] and follows the two-view geometry approach described in [45]. This method finds the camera motion parameters camera motion parameters R and t as shown in Figure 4.

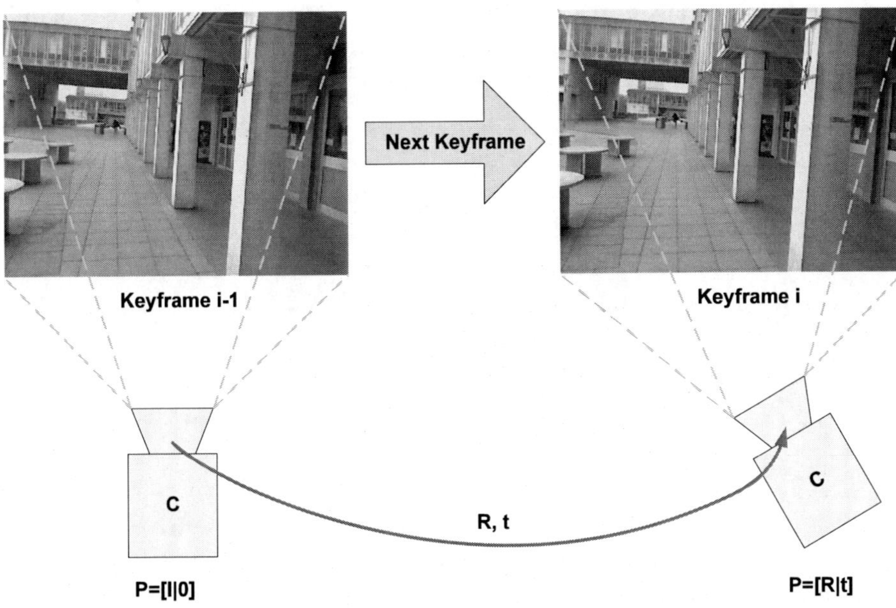

Figure 4. Motion parameters for camera.

When a keyframe $keyframe_i$ is obtained, it is then used to calculate the motion of the camera since the previous keyframe $keyframe_{i-1}$. For this purpose, first the feature point correspondences between these two keyframes are obtained from the correspondences that were already calculated to extract the most recent keyframe using the algorithm of Section 3.1.2.

These correspondences have a normalizing transformation [53] applied to them, which is obtained by first calculating the translation which moves the points around origin and then applying a scaling transformation so that the mean distance of points to the origin $(0, 0)$ will be $\sqrt{2}$. This transformation is given as

$$T_{norm} = \begin{bmatrix} s_t & 0 & -s_t\bar{x} \\ 0 & s_t & -s_t\bar{y} \\ 0 & 0 & 1 \end{bmatrix} \tag{1}$$

where s_t is the scaling parameter which is calculated using the distances of features to the origin while $\bar{x}$ and $\bar{y}$ are the coordinate averages. This transformation is applied to the features in both $keyframe_i$ and $keyframe_{i-1}$. This normalizing transformation is an important step since it affects the conditioning of the matrices used in calculating the fundamental matrix [45]. The transformation is calculated separately for both of the keyframe features and it can be seen that a more uniform distribution of the features is obtained as a result of the transformation which is important for the accuracy of the homography matrix calculated from these features, following our findings in [54].

Following this normalization, the fundamental matrix F, which defines the two-view geometry, was calculated using these normalized coordinates. The calculated fundamental matrix was denormalized using

$$F_{denorm} = T_i F T_{i-1} \tag{2}$$

where T_{i-1} and T_i are the normalizing transformations for keyframes $i-1$ and i respectively.

Before calculating the essential matrix [44] E, it is important to make sure that F satisfies the rank-2 constraint (F having zero determinant) since this motion estimate is sensitive to noise from small motion and feature points that yield a degenerate surface *e.g.,* a plane in 3D [55]. This is done (following the approach described in [55]) by first calculating the SVD of F as $F = USV^T$. The next step is setting the last element of S matrix (*i.e.,* $S_{3,3}$) to 0. Finally, F is recreated using the multiplication of this modified S: USV^T.

When the camera calibration K is known, the essential matrix E can be calculated from the fundamental matrix [45] using

$$E = K^T F K \tag{3}$$

Using E, the motion parameters can be obtained up to scale and with some uncertainty using the approach described in [45]. This will result in more robust computations [52] due to known camera calibration. The uncertainty arises from the existence of four possible solutions for R and t. These solutions indicate four possibilities in which the position of features differ relative to the camera position.

For this purpose, the following two matrices known as Hartley matrices [45] are defined as

$$W = \begin{bmatrix} 0 & -1 & 0 \\ 1 & 0 & 0 \\ 0 & 0 & 1 \end{bmatrix} \quad Z = \begin{bmatrix} 0 & 1 & 0 \\ -1 & 0 & 0 \\ 0 & 0 & 0 \end{bmatrix} \tag{4}$$

where W is an orthogonal matrix ($W^T W = I$) and Z is a skew-symmetric matrix ($Z^T = -Z$). These two matrices will be used to calculate solutions for the camera motion parameters. For this purpose, first the SVD of E is calculated

$$E = USV^T \tag{5}$$

Then, the following intermediate matrices are calculated using the matrices of (4) with U and V orthogonal matrices obtained from (5)

$$T = UZU^T \quad R_1 = UWV^T \quad R_2 = UW^TV^T \tag{6}$$

For R_1 and R_2, the determinant is made positive [56]

$$\begin{aligned} &\text{if } |R_1| < 0 \text{ then } R_1 = -R_1 \\ &\text{if } |R_2| < 0 \text{ then } R_2 = -R_2 \end{aligned} \tag{7}$$

Then, a vector t' is created using elements of the T matrix given in (6)

$$t' = \begin{bmatrix} T_{2,1} \\ T_{0,2} \\ T_{1,0} \end{bmatrix} \tag{8}$$

Now, the four solutions can be obtained as

$$\begin{aligned} P_0 &= [R_1 \mid t'] \\ P_1 &= [R_1 \mid -t'] \\ P_2 &= [R_2 \mid t'] \\ P_3 &= [R_2 \mid -t'] \end{aligned} \tag{9}$$

One of these four solutions will be selected as the motion estimate between the most recent two keyframes; the most appropriate one is found by creating a 3D reconstruction of the feature points and then projecting them onto the images using the projection matrices constructed with these motion parameters (R and t).

3.1.4. Triangulation of Features

The feature points are reconstructed in 3D by triangulation using the method presented in [57]. The method triangulates a feature point using two camera matrices, P_I and P_T, where the former defines the origin for the motion (for $keyframe_{i-1}$) whereas the latter uses the motion parameters of (9) for $keyframe_i$:

$$P_I = K\,[I \mid 0] \tag{10}$$

and

$$P_T = K\,[R \mid t] \tag{11}$$

where K is the calibration matrix.

The initial camera matrix is assumed to be $P_I = [I \mid 0]$ and the motion calculated using the solutions above is relative to this initial point. The next thing to do is to decide on the motion defined by P_T.

An image point is triangulated, using the linear triangulation method of [45], as follows: First the two projection matrices P_I and P_T are created so that the camera calibration is incorporated in the projection matrices. Then each feature is triangulated by creating the following matrix for $j \in (0, 1, 2, 3)$ following the approach of [47]:

$$J = \begin{bmatrix} P_I[2,j]f_{I1_x} - P_I[0,j] \\ P_I[2,j]f_{I1_y} - P_I[1,j] \\ P_T[2,j]f_{I2_x} - P_T[0,j] \\ P_T[2,j]f_{I2_y} - P_T[1,j] \end{bmatrix} \tag{12}$$

In (12), f_{I1_x}, f_{I1_y} and f_{I2_x}, f_{I2_y} correspond to the image positions for a feature f in images 1 and 2 respectively. $P_I[i,j]$ and $P_T[i,j]$ correspond to the element in cell $[i,j]$ of the related projection matrix.

The SVD of J matrix is calculated

$$J = USV^T \tag{13}$$

and 3D position of the triangulated feature (represented by X) is obtained from the last column of V:

$$X = \begin{bmatrix} V[0,3] \\ V[1,3] \\ V[2,3] \\ V[3,3] \end{bmatrix} \tag{14}$$

Once the image points are triangulated between the two views, these 3D points can be used to select one of the solutions produced above. This is done by projecting the 3D points and checking whether they are in front of the camera in both views (P_I and P_T) or not as follows. The projection of X is calculated in both views:

$$\begin{aligned} x_{P_I} &= P_I X \\ x_{P_T} &= P_T X \end{aligned} \tag{15}$$

This projection is then checked to determine whether the z coordinate is positive relative to the cameras:

$$\begin{aligned} x_{P_I}[2,0]\, X[3,0] > 0 \\ x_{P_T}[2,0]\, X[3,0] > 0 \end{aligned} \tag{16}$$

The logic in (16) finds 3D inliers by checking whether a feature has a positive depth relative to the camera (*i.e.,* in front of the camera). The solution resulting in the largest number of inliers is selected as R and t for the final motion estimate.

From the four solutions, it can be seen that P_2 has the largest number of 3D inliers so this solution is selected as the estimated transformation. Projections of the triangulated points have an mean error of 0.20 pixels on both images [58].

3.1.5. Final Motion Estimate

The translation parameters can directly be obtained from t from the selected solution but in order to extract rotations about x, y and z axes from the rotation matrix R, Rodrigues' formula [59] was used. According to this, $R[ij]$ is the corresponding index of the rotation matrix and the rotations are calculated using

$$\begin{aligned} R_y &= \sin^{-1}(R[0,2]) \\ R_x &= \sin^{-1}(-R[1,2])/\cos R_y \\ R_z &= \sin^{-1}(-R[0,1])/\cos R_y \end{aligned} \tag{17}$$

From these found transformations, a transformation matrix is formed as

$$Tr = \begin{bmatrix} \cos R_y \cos R_z & -\cos R_y \sin R_z & \sin R_y & t_x \\ \sin R_x \sin R_y \cos R_z + \cos R_x \sin R_z & -\sin R_x \sin R_y \sin R_z + \cos R_x \cos R_z & -\sin R_x \cos R_y & t_y \\ -\cos R_x \sin R_y \cos R_z + \sin R_x \sin R_z & \cos R_x \sin R_y \sin R_z + \sin R_x \cos R_z & \cos R_x \cos R_y & t_z \\ 0 & 0 & 0 & 1 \end{bmatrix} \tag{18}$$

This transformation is then applied to the last position of the camera stored in homogeneous coordinates. This approach is similar to dead-reckoning [48], where the final position is calculating by adding the estimated displacement to the last known position. As mentioned earlier, a filtering process using KF was used before this transformation matrix was created in order to refine the obtained estimate. This part was removed from the implementation since this result will be combined with results from other sensors in the following section.

3.2. Combining Estimates from Multiple Sensors

A tracking system that will be used for AR applications has two main requirements: accuracy and frame rate (*i.e.*, fps). The first requirement is related to the performance of the pose estimation algorithm and how accurately the tracking system can find the position and orientation of the user in the environment. Accuracy problems of current tracking devices, considering that they are low-cost devices rather than the tactical-grade sensors used in military operations, cause static errors during the motion estimation process. The second requirement is related to dynamic errors (the end–to–end system delay; see Section 2) occurring because of the delay in estimating the motion of the user and displaying images based on this estimate. It is known that the human visual system can process 8–10 images in a second and current industrial standards for frame rate is between 25 and 30 fps [60].

The vision-based user tracking method described in Section 3.1 can provide about four motion estimates in a second which is not fast enough to capture every important motion the user may have performed. In addition to this, the frame rate obtained using the vision-based method as the only estimate is not high enough to provide satisfactory results in the AR application considering the additional time required for rendering and displaying the models. Finally, this motion estimate has an increasing error due to the dead-reckoning approach followed.

For the reasons described above, a sensor fusion approach was followed to provide more accurate estimates of motion more quickly using the high sampling rates of an IMU and GPS. Integration of data from these sensors has been well-studied [61] in order to improve upon the robustness of the individual sensors against a number of problems related to accuracy or drift. The KF is the most widely-used filter due to its simplicity and computational efficiency [62].

The motion estimates obtained by the individual sensors are prone to error due to problems related to accuracy and drift. It makes sense to combine measurements from several sensors in order to exploit their characteristics, which are complementary to each other, in order to yield more accurate results. For this reason a sensor fusion approach was followed using a KF, since it is most common for such applications [62].

The following subsections elaborate on the fusion filter, describing how the motion estimates from the three sensors are combined in a tightly-coupled design, the approach making use of multiple threads for efficiency and finally the tracking system using the sensor fusion algorithm presented here.

3.2.1. Fusion Filter

The filter designed for integration of three sensors consists of a state x which includes positional data ($P = (P_x, P_y, P_z)^T$), linear velocities ($V = (V_x, V_y, V_z)^T$), rotational data ($R = (R_x, R_y, R_z)^T$) and angular velocities ($\Omega = (\Omega_x, \Omega_y, \Omega_z)^T$):

$$x = (P, V, R, \Omega)^T \tag{19}$$

A simple state consisting of 12 elements will facilitate obtaining a better performance in speed than one with a larger state. At each iteration, the predict–measure–update cycle of the KF is executed in order to produce a single output from several sensors as the filter output.

In the first stage, *i.e.*, prediction, a transition matrix (F of (20)) is applied to the state x in order to obtain the predicted position:

$$F = \begin{bmatrix} 1 & 0 & 0 & \Delta t & 0 & 0 & 0 & 0 & 0 & 0 & 0 & 0 \\ 0 & 1 & 0 & 0 & \Delta t & 0 & 0 & 0 & 0 & 0 & 0 & 0 \\ 0 & 0 & 1 & 0 & 0 & \Delta t & 0 & 0 & 0 & 0 & 0 & 0 \\ 0 & 0 & 0 & 1 & 0 & 0 & 0 & 0 & 0 & 0 & 0 & 0 \\ 0 & 0 & 0 & 0 & 1 & 0 & 0 & 0 & 0 & 0 & 0 & 0 \\ 0 & 0 & 0 & 0 & 0 & 1 & 0 & 0 & 0 & 0 & 0 & 0 \\ 0 & 0 & 0 & 0 & 0 & 0 & 1 & 0 & 0 & \Delta t & 0 & 0 \\ 0 & 0 & 0 & 0 & 0 & 0 & 0 & 1 & 0 & 0 & \Delta t & 0 \\ 0 & 0 & 0 & 0 & 0 & 0 & 0 & 0 & 1 & 0 & 0 & \Delta t \\ 0 & 0 & 0 & 0 & 0 & 0 & 0 & 0 & 0 & 1 & 0 & 0 \\ 0 & 0 & 0 & 0 & 0 & 0 & 0 & 0 & 0 & 0 & 1 & 0 \\ 0 & 0 & 0 & 0 & 0 & 0 & 0 & 0 & 0 & 0 & 0 & 1 \end{bmatrix} \tag{20}$$

where Δt is the time between two prediction stages.

The majority of the operations required for integrating the motion estimates from the three sensors are performed in the second stage, where measurements are taken and provided to the filter so that it can update itself. This stage can be examined separately for the position and orientation estimates. For the latter, the output of the IMU filter ($m_R = (yaw, pitch, roll)$ provide the rotational measurements used to update R in (19).

The idea of combining the positional estimates from the camera, GPS and IMU is due to the fact that the GPS is a discrete-time position sensor [62]. In order for the AR system used in applications presented in Section 4 to update the position of the virtual camera more rapidly, the position estimates from the fusion filter need to have smooth transitions between them in order to provide the impression of continuous motion. This is achieved by applying the transformation Tr of (18), obtained from the motion estimate of the camera, to the position provided by the GPS sensor (m_{gps}) and then adding the motion estimate of the IMU (m_{imu}) as an offset:

$$m_P = Tr \times m_{gps} + m_{imu} \tag{21}$$

where m_P constitutes the positional measurements for the fusion filter.

Having all the measurements (m_P and m_R) ready, the filter can now update itself. After the update, the obtained estimates can directly be used by the AR system described later in the paper in order to update the position of the virtual camera.

3.2.2. Multi-threaded Approach

The sensors used in the system had different data rates for delivering data and performing calculations to produce a motion estimate. These frequency differences resulted in a challenge while combining them to generate a single output for the AR system. To elaborate, the vision-based system can produce up to 4 motion estimates per second while the IMU can produce up to 250 samples per second which are to be used for the orientation filter and GPS can produce only a single measurement every second. Furthermore, AR processing has to produce a minimum of 10 fps in order to generate a smooth flow of the display.

A second challenge is due to the execution method of the GPS and the IMU sensors. The library handling these sensors was designed to be event-driven (*i.e.,* an event is triggered each time a datum is available.). The library makes an automatic call the related event handler when data from any of these two sensors become ready. This did not allow the handling of these sensors in the same thread, where other computations are performed in a procedural manner.

Due to the differences in data rates and the application logic used for the sensors employed in the system, a multi-threaded approach was followed as shown in Figure 5. The design used two child threads in addition to the main thread in order to circumvent the challenges mentioned above. The main thread is used to acquire camera images and pass these to both of the vision-based method as keyframes and AR processing. A child thread is used to handle vision-based processing by accessing the camera images acquired. The algorithm generates an estimate which will be later used by the fusion filter in the main thread. A second child thread handles the GPS and IMU sensors and computes the estimate generated by them.

When the child threads have an estimate, they are joined at the fusion filter running in the main thread. The fusion filter produces a single final estimate of position and orientation which will be used as the viewpoint parameters for AR processing along with the image acquired by the camera.

It is also worth mentioning that the design here followed a producer-consumer approach. The child threads are mainly responsible for producing the position/orientation estimate, while the fusion filter consumes these estimates. In order to prevent corruption of data in shared locations (*e.g.*, the camera image or values storing the estimates from vision-based method and other sensors), mutexes [63] were used to prevent cases where the two threads might be competing to access shared information at the same time (*i.e.*, where race conditions occur).

The approach described here may appear as an implementation detail, but is essential if one is to show that the system is working based on the principles laid out in [5] (*i.e.*, using parallelism for performance). This approach resulted in satisfactory frame rates in the final application.

3.2.3. Tracking System

The fusion algorithm was tested on a simple tracking system designed for this study. As shown in Figure 6, the system consists of a laptop computer (Intel, dual core 2.80Ghz, 4GB memory with Linux operating system), a GPS receiver, an IMU and a web camera. An external power supply was also required for the hub connecting the sensors to the laptop since a single port was not able to provide enough power for the three sensors.

The placement of the sensors was chosen considering the lever-arm effect [64] which occurs particularly in GPS–IMU integration systems when sen-

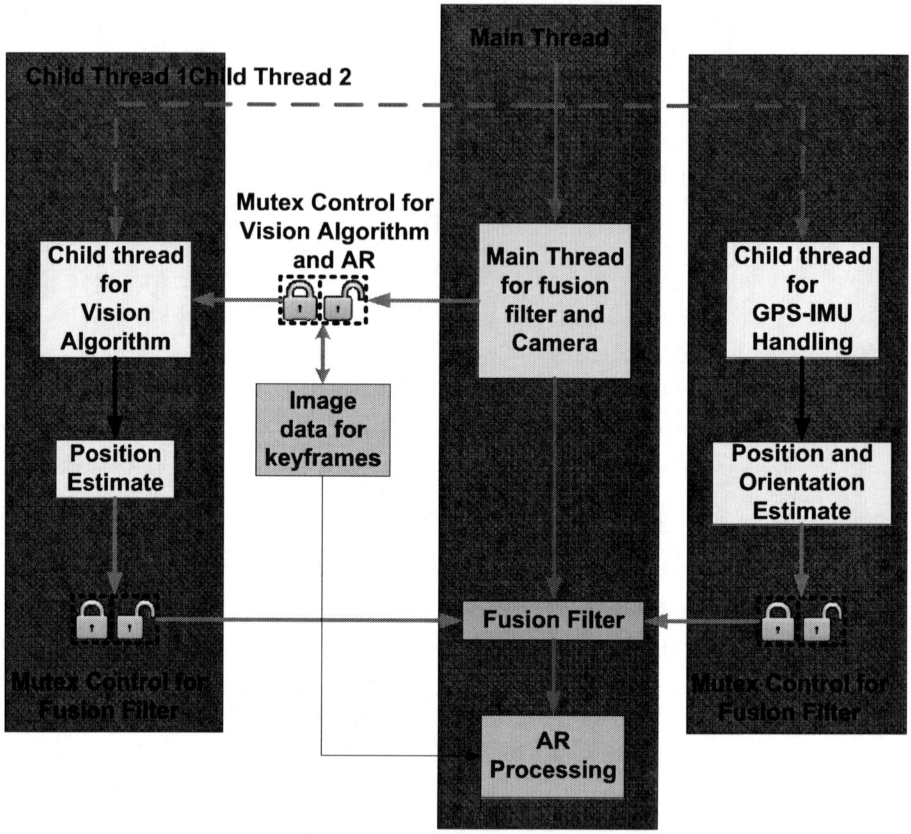

Figure 5. Diagram of using multiple threads to access data from different sensors. The main thread is responsible for acquiring camera images, the fusion filter and using these two generating the AR output. The GPS and IMU handler is handled by a child thread since it is working based on events generated by these two sensors. The second child thread is responsible for the vision algorithm. Race conditions are prevented using three mutexes (shown with locks).

sors are placed apart from each other, so that the positional and rotational data sensed by them correspond to different positions. With this in mind, the camera, IMU and the antenna of the GPS are all placed 2–3 cm apart from each other, a negligible distance.

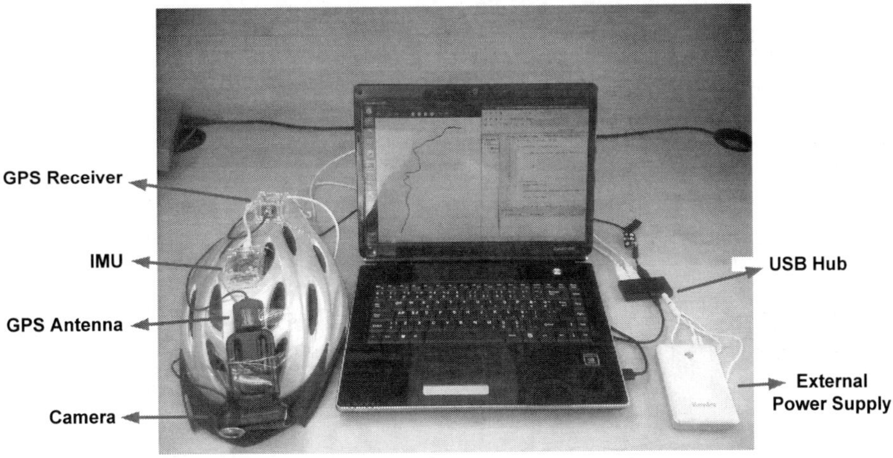

Figure 6. Tracking system.

3.3. Employing Kinect for Accurate Tracking

Microsoft's RGB–depth sensor Kinect [65] provides depth (range using IR light) information along with the RGB image which can be used to generate a 3D point cloud as a representation of the environment as shown in Figure 7.

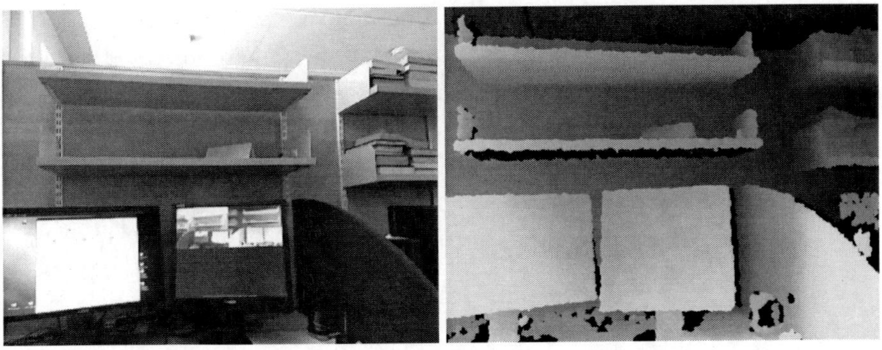

(a) RGB image (b) Depth image

Figure 7. RGB and depth images from Kinect. In (b), objects closer to the sensor are shown with a brighter yellow while the colour becomes darker for the objects away from the sensor.

With Kinect it is also possible to extract the pose of the camera using the PNP methods described in [66]. This pose can be used as the viewpoint for the virtual camera which will be used for rendering synthetic objects over real-world objects for an *in situ* AR algorithm.

Estimation of the camera pose in 3D is a widely-studied research topic [45, 67, 68], normally obtained using vision-only methods such as the PNP solution, which aims to recover camera pose using the positions of 3D features and their projections. For instance, Tam *et al.* [69] used OpenCV's PNP functionality for real-time AR: In a preliminary (off-line) phase, a map of features was first created from known 3D positions in the real world, with each point being described by a SURF descriptor [70]. Subsequently, an on-line system matched SURF features from the camera to those of the map, and then the camera pose was calculated. The time taken for calculating and matching SURF features is significant, so this had to be performed on a GPU.

Sensing the colour and depth of a scene concurrently with Kinect allows extracting the 3D structure of the surrounding and creating a representation of the environment. The use of Kinect data with the PNP algorithm has also been investigated [71] for image-based registration. The analysis involved determining relative and absolute accuracies of the Kinect and another sensor according to the camera pose obtained from the E-PNP algorithm [72].

Kinect returns an RGB image along with a depth image which are not perfectly aligned due to the disparity between the sensors, see [73] for details on this. In order to find correspondences, first the values from the depth image must be back-projected into 3D coordinates and then projected onto the RGB image. Figure 8 illustrates this process.

3.3.1. Detecting Features for *In Situ* Augmentation

The performance of the plane extraction algorithm described in [73] was far from real-time, even for a simple application. For this purpose, rather than trying to extract planar features from a large set of 3D points, the approach described here used was matching features from the environment in order to track the camera pose and use simple rectangle detection from the RGB images [66]. The reason behind this approach is that, irrespective of whether columns are cylindrical or fluted, their projection in the 2D image will be rectangular, and such shapes are relatively easy to detect.

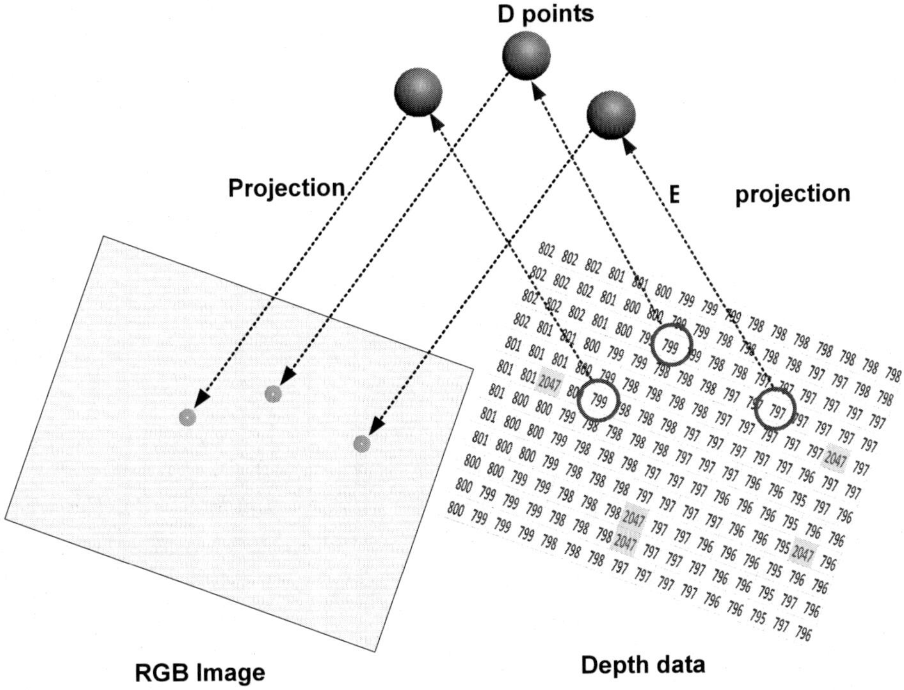

Figure 8. Back-projection of depth data and projecting 3D points; shaded values (red) in the depth data show unreliable raw disparities.

Storing 3D–2D Correspondences. The 3D points resulting from the back-projection of the depth sensor and their corresponding projection points are stored in a data structure once they are calculated. This data structure, shown in Table 1, allows the 3D position ($\mathbf{p}$) corresponding to a 2D pixel (p''') to be obtained quickly.

Efficiency is important when accessing this map of correspondences since it will be used for two purposes: estimating camera pose and finding the coordinates of detected rectangles in 3D.

Finding Camera Pose. The camera position must be found relative to the 3D points obtained from the Kinect sensor, and that is best performed by tracking reliable image features over several frames. The set of points used for tracking

Table 1. Data structure to store point data

Index	Data
$\langle p'''_{x_0}, p'''_{y_0} \rangle$	$\mathbf{p}_0$
$\langle p'''_{x_1}, p'''_{y_1} \rangle$	$\mathbf{p}_1$
$\vdots$	$\vdots$
$\langle p'''_{x_n}, p'''_{y_n} \rangle$	$\mathbf{p}_n$

needs to be stable in order to achieve robust localization of the camera.

To achieve this, the FAST feature detector [74] was used to find features in the RGB image. This detector produces features that are repeatable [75] and widely scattered across the image [76], important characteristics if the resulting homography matrix is to be accurate (see the discussion in [54]), and fast if the system is to operate at video rate. The keypoints obtained from FAST were described using the BRIEF descriptor [77], which is also known to be robust and operate at video rate. The binary structure of the BRIEF descriptor allows two descriptors to be matched using *XOR* instructions, and is therefore rapid to execute.

After the initial set of features has been obtained, these points are matched against the features detected in subsequent frames, outliers being rejected using RANSAC. 3D information for matched points is obtained from the data structure (Table 1) alluded to in the previous subsection. There can be cases where a pixel position may not have an associated 3D entry in the table, perhaps due to reflection of the IR beam or an alignment problem because of the disparity between the depth sensor and camera; when this happens, the closest 2D point in the data structure is used and the corresponding depth calculated as the mean of depths within a 21×21-pixel region.

Algorithms for calculating the position and orientation of the camera are well-established [78], [68], provided that the intrinsic parameters (focal length *etc.*) are known through calibration. Correspondences between 3D points and their 2D projections are used in order to recover the camera pose. The corresponding 2D and 3D points stored in Table 1 are used to calculate the camera position using a recent PNP solution known as EPNP [72], [79] as the initial estimate.

As discussed in [68, 66], PNP solutions are easily affected by noise, and this manifests itself as an unpleasant jittering of the camera position and hence rendered imagery. To reduce this, the estimate of the camera pose is filtered. As will be shown below, a sliding window filter of size 15 reduces this effect but does not eliminate it, while a KF [80] was found to be more effective. The state of this filter comprises the x, y, z coordinates of the camera position and their velocities V_x, V_y and V_z. Measurements of (x, y, z) are obtained from the EPNP algorithm discussed above. The velocities were initialized to $0.5\ units/frame$ for the three axes, reasonable for a user standing and observing ancient ruins (*i.e.,* little or no motion). The transition matrix F is given as

$$F = \begin{bmatrix} 1 & 0 & 0 & \Delta t & 0 & 0 \\ 0 & 1 & 0 & 0 & \Delta t & 0 \\ 0 & 0 & 1 & 0 & 0 & \Delta t \\ 0 & 0 & 0 & 1 & 0 & 0 \\ 0 & 0 & 0 & 0 & 1 & 0 \\ 0 & 0 & 0 & 0 & 0 & 1 \end{bmatrix} \tag{22}$$

At each frame, first the transition matrix F is applied to the current camera position as the prediction step (Δt is the time passed between two consecutive frames). Then the measurements for the camera pose calculated using EPNP are used to refine this prediction for updating the filter, and the state is used for the viewpoint of augmentation. It was found that this filter reduced jittering to the point where it was imperceptible.

Detecting Objects for Augmentation. After determining the camera pose, the next step is to find planar objects— to be augmented, in this work, by synthetic column models as shown in the applications in Section 4.2. The approach presented here first finds rectangular features in the scene using the RGB images instead of the 3D planes [73]. The detected rectangles were filtered based on their sizes and orientations. Finally, a PF was used to track the extracted rectangles since some of them could not be detected in all frames.

For the RGB image, any visual noise was reduced by Gaussian smoothing [81]. Then the Canny edge detector [82] was applied to each of the colour channels independently. Contours were extracted from the edge images using an approximation method [83]; contours that contain four vertices with angles between pairs of lines joining these vertices close to 90° form reliable rectangles as depicted in Figure 9. Small rectangles and rectangles having inappropriate aspect ratios (vertical columns are required for this application) were rejected.

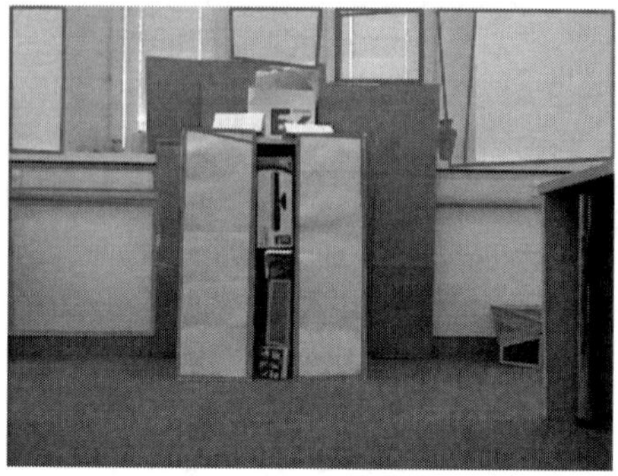

Figure 9. Rectangular features located within an image.

The rectangles detected using the method described above tend to disappear and re-appear from frame to frame due to the changes in lighting conditions. For this reason, the centres of the rectangles were tracked using the *Condensation* algorithm [84].

The state of the filter is initialized with the centre coordinates of a detected rectangle and a set of particles were initialized randomly within the 20-pixel radius of the centre. In the following frames, each time the same rectangle is detected, the centre coordinates of the newly detected rectangle (still the same rectangle tracked with small variations in the centre location) are used to update the particle weights. The number of particles for the algorithm was selected as $N = 50$, which was found to be sufficient (*i.e.,* not causing particle deprivation [85]). At each frame, the particles are updated using the result of the rectangle detection algorithm described above, resulting in the centre of the rectangle being tracked robustly as depicted in Figure 10. After the re-sampling update is performed, the particle with the largest weight is selected both for augmentation and propagation into the next state.

The 3D position of each rectangle's centre, tracked by the PF mentioned, will be retrieved from the map in Table 1 and column models will be rendered at these 3D positions as an interesting AR application in Section 4.2.

The complete augmentation algorithm is given in Algorithm 1.

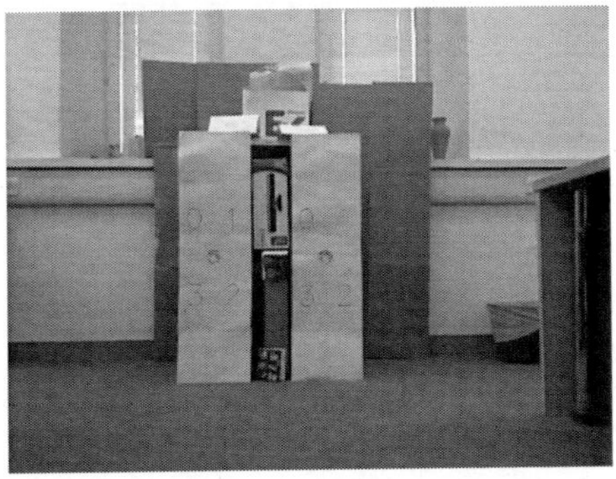

Figure 10. Tracking selected rectangles. Small green circles show the estimates of their centres whereas the large dark blue circle is the particle with largest weight.

3.3.2. Identifying Body Parts

Another interesting application of Kinect is due to its human-skeleton tracking capabilities which is done by detecting the user in the depth image and then finding joint positions by inferring the skeleton pose using a decision forest [86]. The OPENNI NITE library [87, 88] processes depth information from Kinect and performs detection of body parts as shown in Figure 11.

(a) A standing user in the calibration pose—see discussion in the text

(b) A jumping user

Figure 11. User tracking with Kinect.

Algorithm 1 *In-situ* augmentation

Require: I_C: RGB image, I_D: Depth image, 3D models for augmentation.
  Load models and camera calibration parameters.
  Initialize the KF and rendering environment.
  for all frames **do**
    if first frame **then**
      Extract the initial set of features for tracking using FAST detector and BRIEF descriptor.
      Find the initial number of rectangles for augmentation, initialize the PF.
    else
      Compute 3D points from the depth data.
      Calculate projections and create the point map.
      Find feature matches by detecting, describing and matching features from the RGB image for the new frame.
      Calculate camera pose using EPNP.
      Update the KF for camera pose using measurements and set viewpoint for augmentation.
      Detect rectangular objects.
      Update PF.
      Retrieve centre coordinates for augmentation.
      Render the view.
    end if
  end for

User tracking can be accurately performed if the user is standing in front of the Kinect sensor (2.5m is given as an ideal distance) with his/her body (the upper body in particular) inside the FOV and not occluded [88].

In the initialization of the skeleton tracking algorithm, a calibration is automatically performed for improved accuracy in the user position. At this stage, the user is expected to stand in the calibration pose, referred to as "Psi" (Ψ), as shown in Figure 11(a). Once, the user pose is obtained successfully, then each joint's position and orientation can be retrieved. It is also noted that the accuracy for joint positions is higher than for orientations [88]. A confidence value is provided by the library as an indicator of how well the tracking algorithm is progressing.

From the 31 joints that can be tracked with Kinect, three joints were used in this study: the head, torso and right hand as shown in Figure 12.

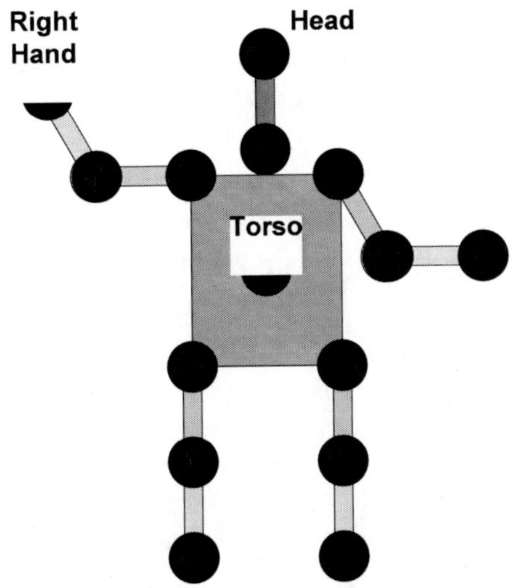

Figure 12. Skeleton joints identified by Kinect.

As each joint is recognized by the library, its position and orientation are returned. These transformations are absolute, not relative, and so can be used directly for rendering, with the exception that the rotation matrix for orientation must be converted to a rotation vector using Rodrigues' formula given in (17).

This skeleton tracking capability will be used for augmenting participants with a *galea* (Roman helmet), toga and sword in an AR application in Section 4.2.

4. Applications

Using the algorithms described in earlier sections, this section presents 3 AR applications for cultural heritage after the rendering process is described.

4.1. The Rendering Pipeline

A rendering environment is needed so that these models can be displayed on top of camera images acquired in real time according to the current position of the user. The following subsections will elaborate on how this is achieved.

4.1.1. Graphics Engine and Scene Graph

Rendering is performed using the Irrlicht [89] game engine, which is an open source, real-time 3D engine. The engine uses a scene graph and provides support for a range of different file formats for loading and displaying the models created in the previous section.

In order to use the game engine, one first needs to initialize the graphics device parameters. An important point here is to set the dimensions of the graphics devices the same size as the input images as this yields better results when graphics are rendered on the camera images.

The engine employs a scene manager, which is basically a scene graph; and this manager is responsible for rendering the content. The scene graph shown in Figure 13 has separate nodes for the camera, 3D meshes (models) and lighting.

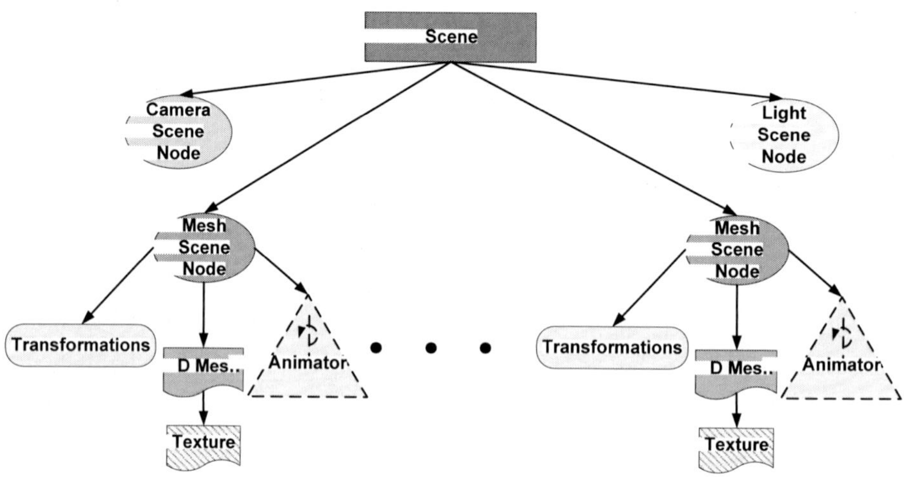

Figure 13. Scene graph structure. A scene can consist of many nodes including cameras, lights and meshes which can have child nodes for transformations, texture and animations.

The camera scene node is derived from Irrlicht's First Person Shooter type camera. The main reason behind this is that this camera can update its target vector automatically when the position and orientation of the camera is updated using the camera pose-finding algorithms presented in Sections 3.1 and 3.3. It is also worth mentioning that this type of camera is normally handled by mouse input; this feature of the camera was disabled so that the update will only be based on the results of the algorithms presented.

The second important component of the scene graph is the mesh scene node, which stores information about a 3D model. Each model has *mesh* and *texture* files created [3]. The *transformation* element of the mesh scene node describes the absolute position and orientation of the model in the scene. The meshes used in the applications can be classified into two groups, namely static and animated meshes. For instance, building models are static meshes whereas coins in the AR game are animated meshes. Meshes in the latter group have an optional *animator* element. This element allows the meshes to rotate about their axes autonomously as an additional effect.

4.1.2. Rendering on Camera Images

When using optical-see-through displays, images from the real environment are obtained automatically using a mirror in the display device and when the graphics are rendered, the augmentation comes at no cost [38]. However, when using video-see-through displays or a camera as the input source, as in this work, the images of the real environment must also be rendered together with other graphics in order to produce the final image. This required a common format which can then be used to view both images, and the approach adopted was to convert camera images to the texture format of the game engine. Raw pixel data of the source image was copied into the format of the target image. At each call to the function drawing the whole scene, first the camera image is rendered and then the game elements are rendered on top of it.

4.1.3. Audio

The AR game presented in section 4.4 plays a simple sound when the user reaches and collects an item. These sounds were played using SDL, a multimedia library which is used to access low-level devices such as the graphics card or the audio driver. This is achieved by first initializing the library for its audio subsystem. Next, the SDL mixer is initialized using the frequency (44100), format (AUDIO_S16SYS), number of channels (2) and chunk size (2048) parameters. Finally, the audio file in WAV format is loaded.

4.2. Application I: Kinect-Derived *In Situ* Augmentation

In the first AR application developed for cultural heritage, objects and users in the environment are augmented using column models and clothing appropriate to a specific age's fashion trends respectively.

The viewpoint required for augmentation is calculated using the approach described in Section 3.3 which uses the Kinect sensor to obtain 3D–2D feature correspondences. These correspondences are used to obtain an initial estimate of the camera pose and then this initial estimate is refined using a KF for additional stability. With the viewpoint information obtained, rectangular features in the image are identified and augmented with columns: this is a common requirement in cultural heritage reconstructions in the eastern Mediterranean, as shown in Figure 1.

The models created for this application are presented in Figure 14. The optimization step during the modelling resulted in a $10-25\%$ reduction in the number of faces for the models. Usually, the more complex the model is, the higher the proportion of faces that can be removed without a noticeable change in appearance; here, these optimizations were most efficient in terms of removing faces for the *galea* model (Figure 14(a)) due to its roughly spherical shape (many faces are required for a smooth surface, hence many can be removed during optimization) whereas the column (Figure 14(e)) was unable to accommodate the removal of many vertices without losing detail of the capital (top) or pediment (base) which can be seen in the columns.

To illustrate the augmentation algorithms presented above, an application was developed to augment rectangular regions of a specific size and aspect ratio in the Kinect imagery. When the camera position and orientation had been found and the centres of suitable rectangles identified, the 3D column models were rendered in front of them. When rectangles were found at a particular distance apart, a further model could be placed above the columns to form an arch, as shown in Figure 15.

The result of augmenting users is shown in Figure 16(a) for a single user and in Figure 16(b) for two users. The general effect is acceptable for toga and sword but minor registration errors are apparent for the galea model in the case of a single user. These registration errors become more severe when multiple users are present, and this appears to be due to the accuracy of skeleton tracking decreasing when the user is not centred in the field of view.

Due to the use of the FAST detector with the BRIEF descriptor, the complete

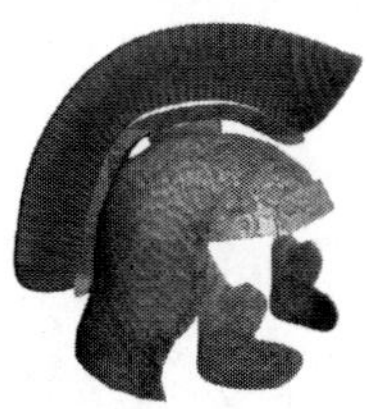

(a) *Galea* (Roman helmet)

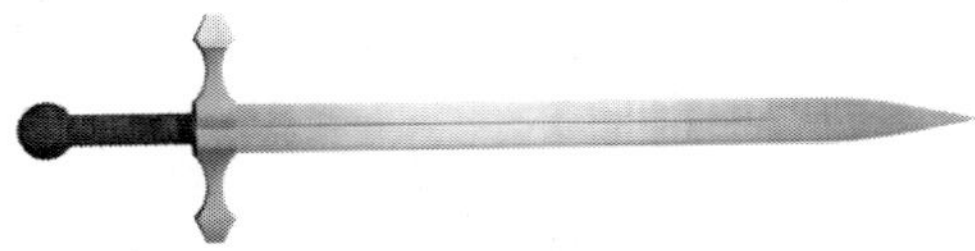

(b) Sword

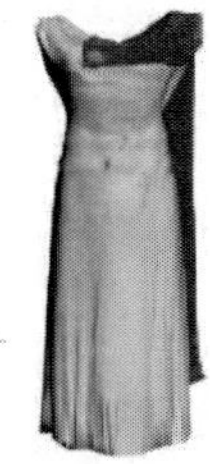

(c) Toga

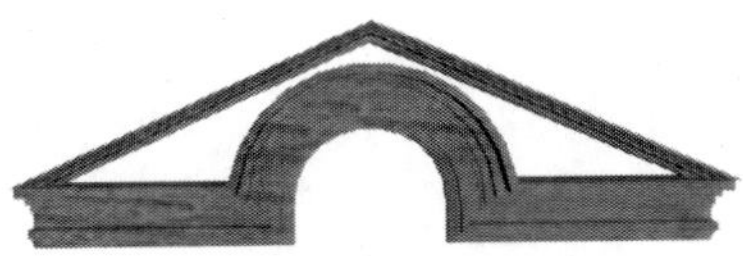

(d) Top arch

(e) Column

Figure 14. Models created for the augmenting participants.

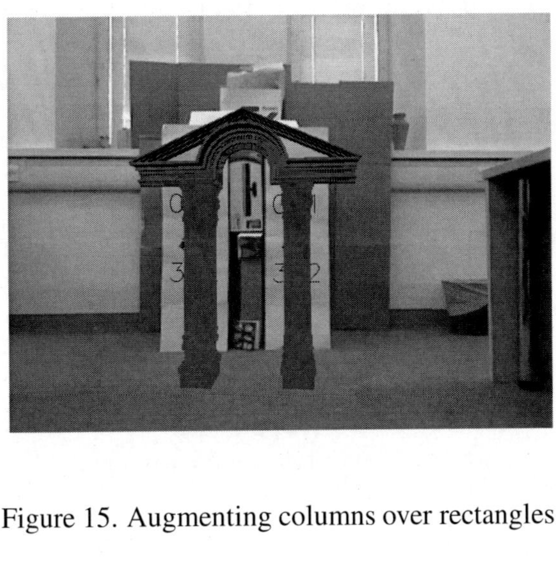

Figure 15. Augmenting columns over rectangles.

(a) Augmenting a single user with toga, galea and sword

(b) Augmenting two users

Figure 16. Augmenting participants.

augmentation process which can run at video rates (25fps).

4.3. Application II: A Visit to Ancient Ephesus

The second application presented here allows a user walk inside a large AR model of the State *Agora*, shown in Figure 17, in the ancient city of Ephesus, located in Turkey. The application makes use of the localization algorithm developed in Section 3.2 to allow a user's motion in real world to be reflected in the application.

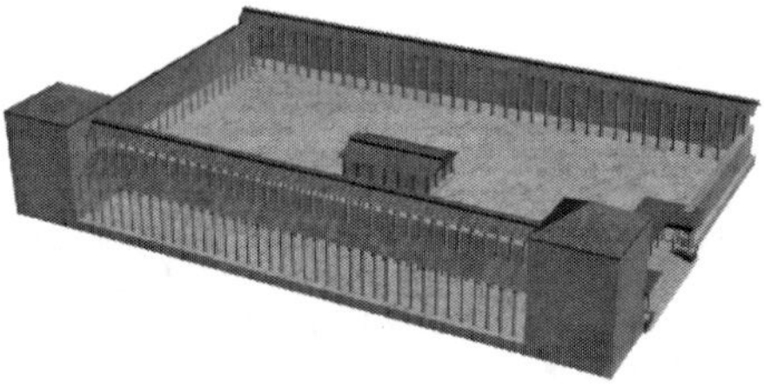

Figure 17. State *Agora* model.

As can be seen, the model includes a large number of columns which follow the Ionic design [90] (*i.e.,* with scrolls on the capitals). Such a high number of models with significant amount of detail add to the time required for rendering the scene. Initial versions of the applications ran at 2–3fps, which was obviously unsatisfactory. The application's frame rate benefited from the following improvements:

1. Use of different threads for the module working for the vision-based algorithm and the module handling the GPS and IMU inputs to separate them from the fusion algorithms and the augmentation part have significantly improved the frame rate.

2. Optimization of different parts of the model have reduced the number of faces to be drawn facilitating a higher frame rate. Especially columns which are abundant in the scene and have fine detail due to the rolled structure of the capital were introducing a significant number of faces before the optimization was performed.

3. Division of the complete model into five parts as shown in Figure 18 helped storing these parts separately in the scene graph. The rendering engine will not render the parts of the scene graph which are not inside camera's viewing frustum.

Following these improvements, the frame rate increased to 16fps which is still less than the de facto standards of 25–30fps yet providing an acceptable frame rate. The third optimization in particular allowed the frame rate to remain stable during display: frequent changes in frame rate according to the changing number of faces visible in the scene makes for a poor experience. The base of the middle part of Figure 18 was also removed in order to place the model on the ground.

Tracking is achieved on a laptop computer with the user wearing a helmet instrumented with a camera, GPS and an IMU as shown in Figure 19. The augmentations are displayed on the screen rather than an HMD.

Figure 20 presents views from the developed application. The user interface for this application is quite simple, just displaying the name of the model and the current frame rate.

4.4. Application III: An AR Game – Treasure Hunt

The final application is an AR game, which again works using the tracking system (Section 3.2). The aim of the game is to collect items and direct the user

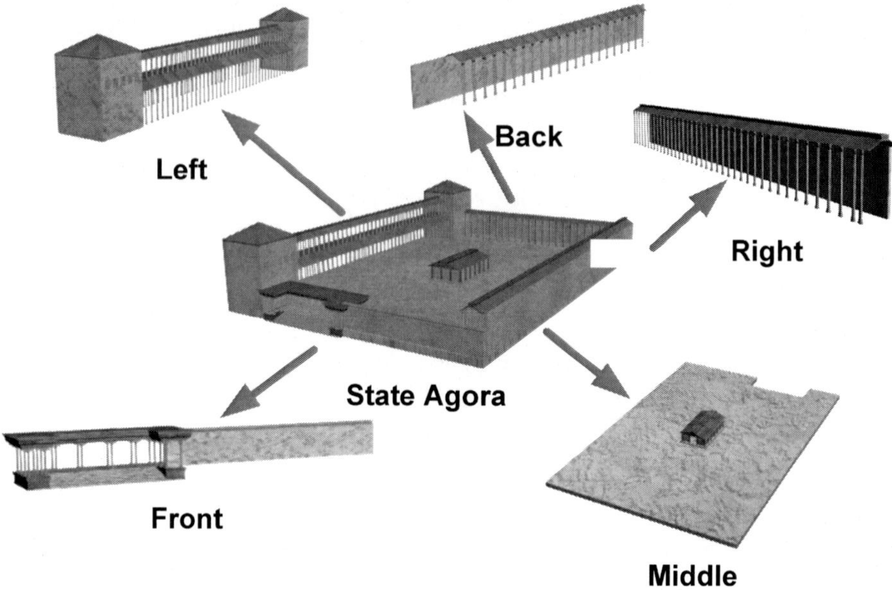

Figure 18. Division of the State *Agora* model for the scene graph.

Figure 19. User wearing the tracking system and displaying the models.

(a) Entering through the gate (b) Inside the *Agora*

Figure 20. Views from the AR application.

to close a loop within the AR context, albeit unconsciously.

As with previous applications, the game presents an egocentric view of the environment. The rules of the game are quite simple: the user needs to reach and collect all the reward items available as quickly as possible. When he or she reaches an item, the score is incremented by an amount that depends on the type of item encountered. The game provides three types of items: small coins, large coins and a chest (Figure 21), with rewards of 10, 30 and 50 points respectively.

After the game is initialized with the positions of all items set, the game loop starts. The coin models use the animator and they rotate about their axes while the chest models remain static. At each frame, the position of the user is checked against the item positions by calculating the distance between them. If this distance is less than some threshold value (done so that there is some tolerance against positioning inaccuracies), then the score is updated, the item is set as "hit" and a sound file is played as described in section 4.1.3. The items collected by the user simply disappear. A timer is used for two purposes. First, it is constantly updated in the display to provide feedback to the user. It is also used to decay the score

$$score = initialScore \times c/time \tag{23}$$

where $score$ is the final score to be added and $initialScore$ correspond to the rewards mentioned above. The constant c is selected as 5.0 arbitrarily. This forces the user to collect the game tokens quickly.

(a) Chest

(b) Coin

Figure 21. Models used in the AR game.

Views from the AR game are presented in Figure 22. The game has an interface which displays the score and time passed making the game more challenging and hence interesting. Figure 22(b) shows that the game can also be played with the AR reconstruction of the State *Agora*. Note the frame rate of the game is higher when the game is displayed on its own (*i.e.,* without the reconstruction).

5. Conclusion

Application of AR to cultural heritage is a fascinating research topic. It allows preserving the original building structures, already subject to wear and tear over hundreds of years, and provide an entertaining way of learning their history by seeing the original building structures instead of ruins.

Apart from creating accurate models of the ancient buildings, the most important part in developing such applications is performing the user tracking (*i.e.,* finding their position and orientation in the environment) accurately.

The keyframe based localization algorithm presented in Section 3.1 used two-view geometry to estimate the motion of the user and achieved more promising results in terms of tracking. This method was able to track the overall motion but missing some fine details due to vision processing.

(a) User collecting reward items

(b) The game can be played inside the State *Agora*.

Figure 22. Views from the AR game.

Considering the operation in outdoor environments, the aid of the GPS and IMU sensors was exploited in a sensor fusion framework in order to achieve more accurate tracking results in Section 3.2. The sensor fusion algorithm combined the position and rotation measurements from the camera, GPS and IMU to produce a single estimate for the user pose. The additional data processing did not add to the computation time; indeed, it was reduced due to the design making use of multiple threads. This allowed the system to capture the motion of the user more accurately for cases where he or she walks at varying speeds or stands, an important feature for a user walking around an ancient site and frequently stopping to examine the ruins.

The recently launched Kinect sensor was also exploited for both tracking the user, using its skeleton-tracking capabilities, and finding the camera position using natural features, using its depth sensor, in the environment for *in situ* augmentation as described in Section 3.3. Such a setup deployed in exhibits will obviously improve the visiting experience in museums.

Using the user tracking system for outdoor environments as well as the camera motion estimation and user tracking features of the Kinect sensor, three applications were presented in Section 4. The first one was for viewing ancient columns augmented over natural features and augmenting users with clothing from ancient ages. The second application allowed the user to view a model of a State *Agora* and walk around it. The final application was a simple AR game in which the user has to collect all the reward items (coins and chests) in the same context as the second application.

The contributions presented in this paper are as open to further improvement as any other piece of research. The AR application presented in Section 4.4 can display a large ancient building along with a simple game making the application more interesting. This can be further improved by creating an animated/live environment using the AR agents presented [91] in order to provide information in cultural heritage context.

References

[1] W. Alzinger and Austria) Osterreichisches Archaologisches Institut (Vienna. *Die Ruinen von Ephesos*. Koska, 1972.

[2] F. Hueber, S. Erdemgil, and M. Buyukkolanci. *Ephesos*. Zaberns Bildbande zur Archaologie. von Zabern, 1997.

[3] B. Koyuncu and E. Bostanci. Virtual reconstruction of an ancient site: Ephesus. In *Proceedings of the XIth Symposium on Mediterranean Archaeology*, pages 233–236. Archaeopress, 2007.

[4] E. Bostanci. Augmented reality applications for cultural heritage. *Pamukkale Universitesi Muhendislik Bilimleri Dergisi*, 17(3):133–142, 2011.

[5] E. Bostanci, N. Kanwal, S. Ehsan, and A. F. Clark. User tracking methods for augmented reality. *International Journal of Computer Theory and Engineering*, 5(1):93–98, 2013.

[6] S.O.H. Madgwick, R. Vaidyanathan, and A.J.L. Harrison. An efficient orientation filter for inertial measurement units (IMUs) and magnetic angular rate and gravity (MARG) sensor arrays. Technical report, Department of Mechanical Engineering, 2010.

[7] R.T. Azuma. A survey of augmented reality. *Presence:Teleoperators and Virtual Environments*, 6:355–385, 1997.

[8] D. Chekhlov, A.P. Gee, A. Calway, and W. Mayol-Cuevas. Ninja on a plane: Automatic discovery of physical planes for augmented reality using visual slam. In *IEEE International Symposium on Mixed and Augmented Reality*, 2007.

[9] G. Klein and D. Murray. Parallel tracking and mapping for small ar workspaces. In *Proceedings of the 2007 6th IEEE and ACM International Symposium on Mixed and Augmented Reality*, pages 1–10, 2007.

[10] G. Bleser. *Towards Visual-Inertial SLAM for Mobile Augmented Reality*. PhD thesis, Fachbereich Informatik der Technischen Universitt Kaiserslautern, 2009.

[11] M. Pupilli. *Particle Filtering for Real-time Camera Localisation*. PhD thesis, Department of Computer Science, University of Bristol, 2006.

[12] G. Klein. *Visual Tracking for Augmented Reality*. PhD thesis, Department of Engineering, University of Cambridge, 2006.

[13] D. Schmalstieg, l G. Schal, D. Wagner, I. Barakonyi, G. Reitmayr, J. Newman, and F. Ledermann. Managing complex augmented reality models. *IEEE Computer Graphics and Applications*, pages 48–57, 2007.

[14] S. Diverdi and T. Hollerer. Heads up and camera down: A vision-based tracking modality for mobile mixed reality. *IEEE Transactions on Visualization and Computer Graphics*, 14:500–512, 2008.

[15] M. Ribo, P. Lang, H. Ganster, M. Brandner, C. Stock, and A. Pinz. Hybrid tracking for outdoor augmented reality applications. *IEEE Computer Graphics and Applications*, pages 54–63, 2002.

[16] G. Bleser, C. Wohlleber, M. Becker, and D. Stricker. Fast and stable tracking for ar fusing video and inertial sensor data. In *International Conferences in Central Europe on Computer Graphics, Visualization and Computer Vision*, 2006.

[17] G. Schweighofer and A. Pinz. Robust pose estimation from a planar target. *IEEE Transactions on Pattern Analysis and Machine Intelligence*, 28:2024–2030, 2006.

[18] E. Mouragnon, M. Lhuillier, M. Dhome, F. Dekeyser, and P. Sayd. Real time localization and 3d reconstruction. In *IEEE Computer Society Conference on Computer Vision and Pattern Recognition*, volume 1, pages 363–370, 2006.

[19] K.W. Chia, A.D. Cheok, and S.J.D. Prince. Online 6 dof augmented reality registration from natural features. In *International Symposium on Mixed and Augmented Reality*, pages 305–313, 2002.

[20] A.J. Davison. Slam with a single camera. In *Concurrent Mapping and Localization*, 2002.

[21] P. Corke, J. Lobo, and J. Dias. An introduction to inertial and visual sensing. *International Journal of Robotics Research*, 28:519–535, 2007.

[22] K. Konolige, M. Agrawal, R.C. Bolles, C. Cowan, M. Fischler, and B. Gerkey. Outdoor mapping and navigation using stereo vision. *Experimental Robotics*, 39:179–190, 2008.

[23] T. Bailey. *Mobile Robot Localisation and Mapping in Extensive Outdoor Environments*. PhD thesis, Australian Centre for Field Robotics, Department of Aerospace, Mechanical and Mechatronic Engineering The University of Sydney, 2002.

[24] G. Schall, E. Mendez, E. Kruijff, E. Veas, S. Junghanns, B. Reitinger, and D. Schmalstieg. Handheld augmented reality for underground infrastructure visualization. *Personal Ubiquitous Computing*, 13:281–291, 2009.

[25] U. Neumann and S. You. Natural feature tracking for augmented reality. *IEEE Transactions on Multimedia*, 1(1):53–64, 1999.

[26] D. Koller, G. Klinker, E. Rose, D. Breen, R. Whitaker, and M. Tuceryan. Real-time vision-based camera tracking for augmented reality applications. In *Symposium on Virtual Reality Software and Technology*, pages 87–94, 1997.

[27] H. Rehbinder and B.K. Ghosh. Pose estimation using line-based dynamic vision and inertial sensors. *IEEE Transactions on Automatic Control*, 48(2):186–199, 2003.

[28] R. Sim, P. Elinas, and J.J. Little. A study of the rao-blackwellised particle filter for efficient and accurate vision-based slam. *International Journal of Computer Vision*, 74(3):303–318, 2007.

[29] M. Fischler and R. Bolles. Random sample consensus: A paradigm for model fitting with applications to image analysis and automated cartography. *Communications of the ACM*, (24):381–395, 1981.

[30] M. Tomono. Monocular slam using rao-blackwellised particle filter with exhaustive pose space search. In *IEEE International Conference on Robotics and Automation*, pages 2421–2426, 2007.

[31] R. Sim, P. Elinas, and M. Griffin. Vision-based slam using the rao-blackwellised particle filter. In *Workshop on Reasoning with Uncertainty in Robotics*, 2005.

[32] P.N. Pathirana, A.N. Bishop, A.V Savkin, S. W. Ekanayake, and T.J. Black. A method for stereo-vision-based tracking for robotic applications. *Robotica*, pages 1–8, 2009.

[33] T. Vidal-Calleja, A.J. Davison, J. Andrade-Cetto, and D.W. Murray. Active control for single camera slam. In *International Conference on Robotics and Automation*, 2006.

[34] J. Civera, A.J. Davison, and J. M. M. Montiel. Interacting multiple model monocular slam. In *International Conference on Robotics and Automation*, pages 3704–3709, 2008.

[35] M. Agrawal, K. Konolige, and R.C. Bolles. Localization and mapping for autonomous navigation in outdoor terrains : A stereo vision approach. In *IEEE Workshop on Applications of Computer Vision*, pages 7–12, 2007.

[36] D. Stricker and T. Kettenbach. Real-time and markerless vision-based tracking for outdoor augmented reality applications. In *International Symposium on Augmented Reality*, 2001.

[37] P. Dahne and J.N. Karigiannis. Archeoguide: System architecture of a mobile outdoor augmented reality system. In *IEEE International Symposium on Mixed and Augmented Reality*, pages 263–264, 2002.

[38] W. Piekarski and B. H. Thomas. Augmented reality working planes: a foundation for action and construction at a distance. In *International Symposium on Mixed and Augmented Reality*, 2004.

[39] P. D. Ritsos. *Architectures for untethered augmented reality using wearable computers*. PhD thesis, Department of Electronic systems Engineering, University of Essex, 2006.

[40] A.H. Behzadan, B. W. Timm, and V. R. Kamat. General-purpose modular hardware and software framework for mobile outdoor augmented reality applications in engineering. *Advanced Engineering Informatics*, 22:90–105, 2008.

[41] T. Oskiper, S. Samarasekera, and R. Kumar. Multi-sensor navigation algorithm using monocular camera, imu and gps for large scale augmented reality. In *Mixed and Augmented Reality (ISMAR), 2012 IEEE International Symposium on*, pages 71–80, 2012.

[42] D. Schleicher, L. M. Bergasa, M. Ocana, R. Barea, and M.E. Lopez. Real-time hierarchical outdoor slam based on stereovision and gps fusion. *IEEE Transactions on Intelligent Transportation Systems*, 10:440–452, 2009.

[43] V. Bonato, J. A. Holanda, and E. Marques. An embedded multi-camera system for simultaneous localization and mapping. *Lecture Notes in Computer Science*, pages 109–114, 2006.

[44] H. C. Longuet-Higgins. A computer algorithm for reconstructing a scene from two projections. *Nature*, 293:133–135, 1981.

[45] R. Hartley and A. Zisserman. *Multiple View Geometry in Computer Vision*. Cambridge University Press, 2003.

[46] E. Royer, M. Lhuillier, Dhome M., and Chateau T. Localization in urban environments: Monocular vision compared to a differential gps sensor. In *IEEE Computer Society Conference on Computer Vision and Pattern Recognition*, pages 114–121, 2005.

[47] A. Geiger, J. Ziegler, and Stiller C. Stereoscan: Dense 3d reconstruction in real-time. In *IEEE Intelligent Vehicles Symposium*, 2011.

[48] Carl Fischer, Poorna Talkad Sukumar, and Mike Hazas. Tutorial: Implementing a pedestrian tracker using inertial sensors. *IEEE Pervasive Computing*, 12(2):17–27, 2013.

[49] J. Sola. *Towards Visual Localization, Mapping and Moving Objects Tracking by a Mobile Robot: a Geometric and Probabilistic Approach*. PhD thesis, lInstitut National Politechnique de Toulouse, 2007.

[50] B. Williams and I. Reid. On combining visual slam and visual odometry. In *Proc. International Conference on Robotics and Automation*, 2010.

[51] G. Bradski and A. Kaehler. *Learning OpenCV: Computer Vision with the OpenCV Library*. O'Reilly, 2008.

[52] T. Tuytelaars, L. Van Gool, L. Dhaene, and R. Koch. Matching of affinely invariant regions for visual servoing. In *Proceedings of the International Conference on Robotics and Automation*, 1999.

[53] R. I. Hartley. In defense of the eight-point algorithm. *IEEE Trans. Pattern Anal. Mach. Intell.*, 19(6):580–593, 1997.

[54] E. Bostanci, N. Kanwal, and A. Clark. Spatial statistics of image features for performance comparison. *Image Processing, IEEE Transactions on*, 23(1):153–162, 2013.

[55] Zhengyou Zhang. Motion and structure from two perspective views: From essential parameters to euclidean motion via fundamental matrix. *Journal of the Optical Society of America A*, pages 2938–2950, 1997.

[56] B. K. P. Horn. Recovering baseline and orientation from essential matrix. *J. Optical Society of America*, 1990.

[57] Richard I. Hartley and Peter Sturm. Triangulation. *Computer Vision and Image Understanding*, 68(2):146–157, 1997.

[58] E. Bostanci, A.F. Clark, and N. Kanwal. Vision-based user tracking for outdoor augmented reality. In *Computers and Communications (ISCC), 2012 IEEE Symposium on*, pages 566–568, 2012.

[59] O. Rodrigues. Des lois géométriques qui régissent les déplacements d'un systéme solide dans l'espace, et de la variation des coordonnées provenant de ces déplacements considérés indépendamment des causes qui peuvent les produire. *Journal de Mathématiques Pures et Appliquées*, pages 380–440, 1840.

[60] P. Read and M.P. Meyer. *Restoration of Motion Picture Film*. Butterworth-Heinemann series in conservation and museology. Elsevier Science, 2000.

[61] P.D. Groves. *Principles of GNSS, inertial, and multi-sensor integrated navigation systems.* GNSS technology and applications series. Artech House, 2008.

[62] E.D. Kaplan and C.J. Hegarty. *Understanding GPS: Principles and Applications.* Artech House mobile communications series. Artech House, 2005.

[63] A. Silberschatz, G. Gagne, and P.B. Galvin. *Operating System Concepts.* Wiley John + Sons, 2013.

[64] J. Seo, J. G. Lee, and C. Park. Leverarm compensation for integrated navigation system of land vehicles. In *Control Applications, 2005. CCA 2005. Proceedings of 2005 IEEE Conference on*, pages 523–528, 2005.

[65] Microsoft Corporation. Kinect for xbox360. http://www.xbox.com/en-GB/Kinect, 2010. Last access: November, 2013.

[66] Erkan Bostanci, Nadia Kanwal, and Adrian F. Clark. Kinect-derived augmentation of the real world for cultural heritage. In *UKSim*, pages 117–122, 2013.

[67] Y. Ma, S. Soatto, J. Kosecka, and Sastry S. S. *An Invitation to 3-D Vision: From Images to Geometric Models.* Springer, 2004.

[68] R. Szeliski. *Computer Vision: Algorithms and Applications.* Springer, 2011.

[69] D. C. C. Tam and M. Fiala. A real time augmented reality system using GPU acceleration. In *Computer and Robot Vision (CRV), 2012 Ninth Conference on*, pages 101–108, 2012.

[70] H. Bay, T. Tuytelaars, and L. V. Gool. SURF: Speeded up robust features. *EECV, LNCS:3951*, pages 404–417, 2006.

[71] M. Weinmann, S. Wursthorn, and B. Jutzi. Semi-automatic image-based co-registration of range imaging data with different characteristics. In *Photogrammetric Image Analysis PIA11, LNCS:6952*, pages 119–124, 2011.

[72] V. Lepetit, F. Moreno-Noguer, and P. Fua. EPnP: An Accurate O(n) Solution to the PnP Problem. *International Journal of Computer Vision*, 81(2):155–166, 2009.

[73] E. Bostanci, N. Kanwal, and A. F. Clark. Extracting planar features from Kinect sensor. In *Computer Science and Electronic Engineering Conference*, pages 118–123, 2012.

[74] E. Rosten and T. Drummond. Machine learning for high-speed corner detection. *Computer Vision-ECCV 2006*, pages 430–443, 2006.

[75] E. Rosten, R. Porter, and T. Drummond. Faster and better: A machine learning approach to corner detection. *IEEE Transactions on Pattern Analysis and Machine Intelligence*, 32:105–119, 2010.

[76] E. Bostanci, N. Kanwal, and A. F. Clark. Feature coverage for better homography estimation: An application to image stitching. In *Proceedings of the IEEE International Conference on Systems, Signals And Image Processing*, 2012.

[77] M. Calonder, V. Lepetit, C. Strecha, and P. Fua. BRIEF: Binary Robust Independent Elementary Features. In *European Conference on Computer Vision*, pages 778–792, 2010.

[78] R. M. Haralick, C. Lee, K. Ottenberg, and Nölle M. Review and analysis of solutions of the three point perspective pose estimation problem. *International Journal of Computer Vision*, 13(3):331–356, 1994.

[79] F. Moreno-Noguer, V. Lepetit, and P. Fua. Accurate non-iterative O(n) solution to the PnP problem. In *IEEE International Conference on Computer Vision*, 2007.

[80] R. E. Kalman. A New Approach to Linear Filtering and Prediction Problems. *Transactions of the ASME Journal of Basic Engineering*, (82 (Series D)):35–45, 1960.

[81] E.S. Gedraite and M. Hadad. Investigation on the effect of a gaussian blur in image filtering and segmentation. In *ELMAR, 2011 Proceedings*, pages 393–396, 2011.

[82] J. Canny. A computational approach to edge detection. *IEEE Transactions on Pattern Analysis and Machine Intelligence*, 8(6):679–698, 1986.

[83] D. Douglas and T. Peuker. Algorithms for the reduction of the number of points required to represent a digitised line or its caricature. *The Canadian Cartographer*, 10:112–122, 1973.

[84] M. Isard and A. Blake. Condensation – conditional density propagation for visual tracking. *International Journal of Computer Vision*, 29(1):5–28, 1998.

[85] S. Thrun, W. Burgard, and D. Fox. *Probabilistic Robotics*. MIT Press, 2006.

[86] J. Shotton, A. Fitzgibbon, M. Cook, T. Sharp, M. Finocchio, R. Moore, A. Kipman, and A. Blake. Real-time human pose recognition in parts from single depth images. In *Computer Vision and Pattern Recognition (CVPR), 2011 IEEE Conference on*, pages 1297–1304, 2011.

[87] OpenNI. OpenNI library. http://openni.org/. Last access: November, 2013.

[88] Inc. PrimeSense. Primesense nite algorithms 1.5, 2011.

[89] Irrlicht. Irrlicht 3d game engine. http://irrlicht.sourceforge.net/. Last access: November, 2013.

[90] B. Evers, C. Thoenes, and Germany) Kunstbibliothek (Berlin. *Architectural Theory: From the Renaissance to the Present : 89 Essays on 117 Treatises*. Midi Series. Taschen, 2003.

[91] E. Bostanci and A. F. Clark. Living the past in the future. In *International Conference on Intelligent Environments, International Workshop on Creative Science*, pages 167–172, 2011.

INDEX

C

D

E

F

G

M

N

O

P

Q

R

S

T

U

V

W

X

Y